The Sixpenny Tiger

Jeanette Taylor Ford

The Sixpenny Tiger © Copyright, Jeanette Taylor
Ford, 2015

Disclaimer:

Whilst certain characters are based on real people; this is a work of fiction and so the character of 'Marjorie' and her family are not based on anyone I know or have known.

In memory of Dorothy Lewis, a special lady.

Also for all the 'aunties' who I worked with and the children we cared for so many years ago.

Acknowledgements:

Thanks once again to my son Tim for doing the technical stuff with the cover.

Special thanks to Sam Parr, artist, for the wonderful cover she has created. Visit Sam on her website: samparr.co.uk

Who knows what goes on behind closed doors?

Or what pain lies behind a smile?

Who understands the night-time terrors

Caused by day-time darkness?

Who cares about those injured ones

Whose scars are within the soul?

Broken bones can mend and become strong again

But it takes unconditional love

To heal a broken heart.

J.T.F.

The Sixpenny Tiger

Chapter 1

Davey

"It wasn't me, Aunty!"

The young boy flinched as she raised her hand.

"Who was it then?" she demanded, "Tell me!"

There was no answer. Brown eyes, filled with tears, looked at her stern face.

"Well – I'm waiting"

Davey knew who had done the deed, but there was no way he was going to tell her. His dad had told him that he had to look after his little brother at all times. He hung his head.

"I knew it – you can't tell me because it was you!" The housemother raised her hand again and, as he flinched away she slapped him round the head. "You're a dirty little boy!"

Davey curled his body on the bed, his arms round his head to try to protect himself as the blows rained down on him. She hit him wherever she could, her hands stinging him through the thin material of his pyjamas.

"I'll teach you to be so dirty – and to lie to me!" she was shouting now, heedless of who might hear.

"WHAT is going on here?" another voice suddenly demanded from the doorway of the bedroom. The matron, not a big woman, but one with a presence, took in the scene before her. Across the room, an even younger boy, Davey's brother, stood by his own bed, watching the shameful scene, fascinated.

Startled, the housemother stopped her screaming and slapping and stood up to face her boss. Her face was red, whether from the exertion or from being discovered brutally hitting one of her small charges, was unclear.

"Davey has wet in the corner of the bedroom again, Mrs Brown and he won't confess that he's done it. He keeps lying to me," she reported.

Emily Brown looked at the weeping child on the bed, then at his little brother standing by, still watching the scene with interest. She had her own suspicions; but she would not say anything in front of these children.

Davey who was now seven, and his little brother John who was six, had come into the care home Emily ran with her husband Albert for the local authority, because their mother had run off with another man, leaving her children behind with their father. He was not able to look after the two boys so they had come into care and had been at the home for about a year now. Emily was a very astute woman; she made it her business to know everything that went on in the home and knew that the smaller boy was treated like a pet by the housemother and her assistant who had charge of this 'family' under their care. However the older boy, Davey, was not so well liked and was often in trouble.

Now, Emily said quietly: "Go and see to the rest of your family, Aunty Marjorie, I will see to things here."

She watched as Marjorie left the room, then she closed the door and turned towards the still curled up little boy on the bed. Then she paused and turned instead towards the younger boy.

"Have you cleaned your teeth John?" she asked him.

He shook his head.

"Then go and do it now – and close the door behind you please," Emily ordered quietly.

John went out of the room slowly, looking at her all the time, and closed the door behind him. Emily waited a few moments, opened the door, checked the hallway outside, then, satisfied John wasn't there, she turned back to Davey. By this time, he had stopped sobbing, although tears still ran down his cheeks. Emily's heart melted as she looked at the little boy before her. He had been through so much already in his short life and he was still suffering.

"Davey, come on child, sit up and let me dry your tears," said Emily, gently taking him by the arm and putting her other arm around him, helped him to sit up. He sat and patiently endured her wiping his face with a couple of tissues she had taken from her pocket. He looked into her face, as she looked into his.

"Tell me Davey, it wasn't you, was it?" she asked.

He mutely shook his head.

"Was it John?"

He looked away from her and stared at his feet dangling from the bedstead. Emily looked at him and sighed.

"Never mind, Davey; I don't expect you to tell on your brother."

Emily patted the child on his head. "Let's get you into bed. Have you been to the bathroom?"

Davey said he had, so she lifted the covers and he climbed into the bed. At that moment, his brother came back into the room and went over to his own bed. He turned round and looked at his brother and for a moment, Davey caught the look of triumph on the younger boy's face....

Emily left the room. She was concerned about this situation between Davey and his housemother. She wondered how the situation could be resolved.

As Marjorie left the boys' room, she was seething inwardly, although making great efforts to hide it and be in control. That woman! How could she come in and more or less show her she was wrong in what she was doing. Matron Wooding would have applauded the discipline that Marjorie was trying to give that boy. He was so insolent! Give her the chance, she would sort him out! This new matron thought she knew everything, but she was soft. You couldn't give these children an inch or they would walk all over you. They would take advantage. They were the scum of the earth, these children; born of parents who were too stupid to bring them up. These people just kept on having babies and then giving them up into care. Something should be done about it. Still, some of the children were all right; it was just that Davey – try as she might, she just couldn't take to him. He, he reminded her of... she shook her head resolutely. "No Marjorie my girl, don't think about it."

As she entered the main family bedroom, she set to getting the children settled and gradually her annoyance began to settle down again. The three little sisters, who slept in this room, were so good and so very cute, even if they did have a mother who didn't seem to know how to stop having babies.

****

As Davey lay in the darkness, his mind floated unwillingly back to his mum. Why did she leave them? What had he done? It must have been his fault, because John was only little. And his dad didn't want them either. He said he couldn't look after them, but didn't he know that Davey would do everything he could to help, just if they could be together? But his dad wouldn't let him. And now they lived in this great big, scary house – he was sure it was haunted!

And worse still, he was being looked after by 'Aunty Marjorie'. As if he wanted to call anyone that horrid 'aunty'! But some of the aunties were okay; Aunty Lillian was nice, it was a pity she wasn't his housemother. Aunty Andrea, who was Aunty Lillian's assistant, was lovely too. But he has to be stuck with Aunty Marjorie. Matron was nice though; he was sorry he couldn't tell her about John, but he had promised. And, he wondered, just what had he done to John to make him want to get him into trouble all the time? He always did his best to look after his brother, just like his dad had told him to.

He thought back to that day when they came home from school to find that his mum wasn't there. His mum and her friend took it in turns to collect the children home from school and it was her friend's turn that day. She had waved to them as they went through their door and went off with her own son.

"Mum! Mum! Where are you?" he called as he went from room to room. There was no sign of her. He didn't know what to do. Dad wouldn't be home for ages yet. He decided to go next door to Aunty Barbara's. She wasn't his real aunt, just a neighbour, but he called her that. He took his brother and went and knocked on her door. When she answered, she said: "Davey, John, what's the matter?"

"Me mum's not there, Aunty Barbara, I don't know where she is. I don't know what to do," explained Davey. He saw the puzzled look on Aunty Barbara's face.

"That's funny. Would you like me to come and look? Perhaps she has left a note somewhere, maybe she's had to go and see someone or help someone. Come on boys, let's go to your house and see."

The boys walked with Aunty Barbara back to their house and followed her inside. Davey watched as she looked around the kitchen and then moved into the living room. Then he noticed, almost at the same time as Aunty Barbara, the note on the mantle behind the clock. It had his dad's name on it. There was another note there too. It had his and John's names on it. Barbara picked it up. Her hand shook as she had begun to fear what it might contain. She handed it to Davey. He looked at it, then slowly opened it and took out the single piece of paper. He didn't read very well yet, he was still only six. He held it out to Aunty Barbara.

"Please will you read it to us?"

She took the note and read slowly:

"Dear Davey and John,

I am sorry but I can't live with you and your dad anymore. I have to go away and I can't take you with me. I'm sorry. I hope you won't hate me. I love you, mum"

Aunty Barbara and the two boys looked at each other; none of them knew what to say. They didn't know what to do. Then Barbara seemed to realise that she was the grown up and she had to take charge.

"Come on boys; let's go back to my house. I will get you something to eat and something ready for your dad. You can watch my television and wait for him."

They followed her back to her house and obediently went into her living room and sat on the floor. She put on the television and they were soon watching the children's programmes. Davey looked engrossed, but he was thinking over and over, "Where are you mum? Why have you gone? What is dad going to do?" He looked at John and he looked as if he didn't care what had happened, in fact he probably didn't understand, after all, he was only five.

When Barbara called them to the table, the boys obediently ate the sausages and mash she had made for them and then went back to watch the television some more. He could see John was looking sleepy and he was getting tired himself, when a knock came at the door. It was his father, distraught, a letter in his hand. He heard him say "she's gone, Barbara, Sue has gone! What am I going to do? How am I going to look after the boys?"

Before he knew it, they were going back to their house and dad was putting them to bed. John started crying for mummy and dad did his best to comfort him, saying she had gone out and he had to be a good boy and go to bed. John calmed down and let dad put him to bed. Davey got himself to bed. He felt as if he was dead and nothing mattered. He just had to do what he was told. He lay awake in his bed and listened to the chink of glass as his father poured drink after drink. After a long time he crept down the stairs and found his father snoring on the sofa, surrounded by empty bottles. It was something he had seen many times. Davey left him there to sleep and went back to bed, but lay awake and troubled. Where was his mum? When would she come back?

They managed for a few days, with Aunty Barbara having the boys after school until Dad came home. Then one day, a woman came to their house to see their dad. The next day, dad told the boys they were not going to school. They were going on a visit to someone and he had packed a case for them as it would be a long visit. Davey was puzzled, but he trusted his dad. They got into the car and dad put the case in the boot. There was only one case and Davey wondered if there were enough things for all three of them for a long stay away from home. They travelled for only about 20 minutes and then they pulled into a gateway, went up a short drive and pulled up in front of a very large grey stone house. There was another car parked there already and when they drew up, the woman who had visited them the previous day got out of the car. She greeted them in a friendly way and then turned to ring the doorbell. In a very few moments the large blue door was opened and there stood the woman he now knew was Auntie Emily. She bade them come in and Davey looked around him as he walked through the door. They were in a very large hallway with a staircase to their right. The woman who had met them was talking to Auntie Emily:

"Mrs. Brown, this is Davey and John and their father Mr. Adams."

"How do you do, Mr. Adams?" Mrs Brown said, shaking his hand. She turned to Davey.

"Hello Davey, hello John. You can call me Aunty Emily. Welcome to Beaumont House. You have come to stay with us for a while. I am going to show you around. It is a big house and you will probably find it a little frightening at first but you will soon find your way around and there are lots of people, adults and children, who will help you."

Davey did indeed soon feel very confused as they were shown room after room, although they were only shown some of the rooms. He saw lots of children around the house of all ages, girls and boys. He was surprised when they went up another set of stairs instead of the big stairs he had seen when they came into the house. When they got to the top of the stairs they were shown a room with three baths in it, which he thought was a bit strange and other rooms with toilets and sinks. Then they walked along the hallway, turned a left corner and went along another hallway until Mrs. Brown stopped at a door. She opened the door and they followed her in.

"This is your bedroom, Davey and John. As you can see, there are only two beds in here. We thought you would be happier sharing a room. Your dad will leave your case here and we will unpack it later."

"Where are you going to sleep dad?" asked Davey. He noticed his dad looked rather uncomfortable. His dad sat on one of the beds and beckoned the two boys to come and sit with him. They sat on the bed with him, one of either side. He put his arms around them.

"Davey and John, you know that your mummy has gone. I have to work and sometimes, as you know, I have to go away for my work. I can't look after you anymore."

"But daddy, we were all right with Aunty Barbara; she will help us until mummy comes back," Davey's eyes were filling with tears. Surely dad wasn't going to leave them here in this big scary house with people they didn't know?

"Son, mummy is not going to come back. And Aunty Barbara can't keep on looking after you for always. It's not fair on her," He nodded towards the woman who had come to see them. "Miss Mason is a Child Care Officer and she feels that you should live here at Beaumont House until there comes a time when I can have you both home again."

Davey was crying now, and, seeing his brother crying, made John cry too. They both clung to their father. Their dad kissed and hugged both his sons. As he hugged Davey, he said, "Be good, my son and always look after your brother; he is only little, he is going to need you to look after him. I will come and see you both as often as I can."

Mrs. Brown indicated that Mr. Adams and Miss Beaumont should leave. They headed for the door.

"Don't go daddy, please don't go!" sobbed Davey and John sobbed along with him. Emily Brown gathered the two boys to her and cuddled them, murmuring that it would be alright and their daddy would be back to see them again soon.

That had been almost a year ago. They had got used to living here now and had formed friendships amongst the other children. But daddy didn't come very often...

Davey shifted himself to a more comfortable position. His skin still hurt where the blows had landed and his head hurt too, from being hit and the crying. He wanted to go home; he wished all this was a bad dream that he would awake from and discover he was still in his own bedroom and mum and dad would be downstairs. But he knew it wasn't a dream, this was his reality. He wondered just how long this hell was going to last for him as he drifted off into a fitful sleep.

Chapter 2.

The Interview

Sarah Louise Golding, paced the floor anxiously.

"Oh mum! Do you think I'll get it?

Sarah, known to everyone as Sally, was very excited. She had an interview! This was not any old interview, this one was for her Dream Job - to work in a children's home. Eighteen year-old Sally had longed to do such a job since she was about fourteen. This was born of the experiences she had had with the young children at a boarding school she attended in those days. The school had some quite young children, some as young as six or seven and those little ones often came to her for comfort when they were missing their mothers. Sally discovered she loved children and decided that this was what she wanted to do. When she still lived in Norfolk, she often visited the National Children's Home, which was just a few miles from her home, learning how it worked and what house parents had to do and how the children lived. There was a calm, loving and peaceful atmosphere there and Sally enjoyed being with them.

However, she also learned that she would need qualifications to work at a NCH home and she didn't even have an 'O' or 'A' level to her name. It seemed that after all, her dreams would not be able to be realised. Then, just a couple of weeks ago, she had seen the advertisement for a Nursery Assistant in the local children's home, Beaumont House – and no qualifications were required!

She had applied for it straight away and to her surprise, she had been given an interview!

"What if they don't like me?" Sally was unable to keep still. There was still an hour before they had to go. She was to have a medical, so her mother was asked to come along as chaperone.

"What if I don't pass the medical?"

Maureen Golding looked at her beloved young daughter. She was also concerned about the medical. Her girl had been a very poorly child with numerous health problems and hearing problems sometimes too. No one knew better than Maureen what Sally had been through, after all, she had been the one who had looked after her throughout the crippling migraines, the asthma, the severe earaches, treated the weeping, open eczema, bullying her not to scratch already very sore skin – but worst of all, the terrible stomach problems.

The school Sally had gone to had been a special school for sick children; she had missed so much mainstream schooling that in the end something drastic needed to be done and so she went off to the boarding school with determination that she was going to 'get on'. Maureen admired her daughter; she had struggled to overcome herself, the ravages that had beset her body and had gained qualifications in typing, which meant she was able to work in an office, although she didn't particularly like it. And she had held a job with Walkers' Nurseries ever since they had moved to Hereford a year ago, before that, in Norfolk, Sally had worked in a solicitor's office.

At five feet two inches, Sally had long dark brown hair, blue eyes and a pale face with a sweet smile. She weighed just seven stone four pounds and looked as if a puff of wind could blow her over. Tiny though she was, and sometimes very poorly looking, people were drawn to her. She loved working at the nurseries; everyone spoke to her as she went by, walking through the nurseries on her way to the offices. It was such a contrast to the Solicitors' office where she had been before, with its dim and dusty interior and moody boss. When the roses were in bloom, one of the nurserymen often gave her bunches of roses to take home for her mum and when it was time for the 'pricking out', Sally would go into one of the large greenhouses and talk to the women as they worked, fascinated by the swiftness of their gentle fingers as they planted the tiny seedlings. When Sally and her parents had moved there the year before, she had badly wanted to work on the nursery with the women, but the boss wanted her to work in his office because she could type his letters for him.

The time came for Sally and Maureen to catch the bus from the bottom of the lane where they lived into town. As she rode in the bus, Sally remembered how she had immediately fallen in love with this place as soon as she saw it. She now never wanted to live anywhere else. She had expected to be homesick for her home town in Norfolk but in fact, she wasn't at all. She had felt an affinity with Hereford and the surrounding area, felt she belonged here. With the Black Mountains in the distance, she thought she had never seen anywhere so beautiful.

Before very long, the bus pulled into the bus station and Sally and Maureen began the walk up the hill towards Beaumont House. After walking for about twenty minutes, they arrived at a large gateway in a stone wall that was only just taller than an average man. They walked up the wide sweeping driveway, eyeing the imposing three storey grey stone house in front of them. It had a large porch, also built of stone. They stood outside the blue studded door. Mother and daughter looked at each other for a moment and then Sally squared her shoulders, took a deep breath and pressed the doorbell. They heard the bell ringing inside. Very shortly, the door opened and a woman with brown curly hair and glasses and a friendly smile invited them to come in.

"Are you Sarah? I am Mrs. Brown and I am the matron of Beaumont House. In a moment you will be introduced to my husband who helps me with the running of the home."

"Yes, I'm Sarah, but everyone calls me Sally Mrs. Brown. I prefer it. This is my mother, Maureen Golding," replied Sally and watched while the two women shook hands.

"Mrs Golding, would you mind waiting in this room here whilst my husband and I have a talk with Sally?" as she spoke, Mrs. Brown opened the door of the room immediately to their left. "This is the Parlour, one of our Family rooms. Please make yourself comfortable," she indicated an armchair by the side of the fireplace. "Would you care for a cup of tea or coffee?"

"Coffee please," replied Maureen. "And don't worry about me, I will be fine."

"I will get someone to bring you a coffee very shortly. Sally, you come with me please." Mrs. Brown went into the hallway again and, seeing a woman at the far end called out: "please would you organise a cup of coffee for Mrs Golding in the Parlour for me, Lillian?" The woman nodded, smiling pleasantly at Sally and disappeared around the corner. Sally followed Mrs. Brown into a room opposite the one her mother was in. It turned out to be an office with a big desk in the centre of the room. A man was sitting in one of the chairs behind the desk. He stood up as they came into the room.

"Sally, this is my husband Mr. Albert Brown. Albert, this is Sarah Golding. She prefers to be called Sally."

Albert Brown was a tall man, mostly bald and wearing glasses. He seemed to Sally that he had a military bearing, and indeed she eventually learned he had been in the army.

Mrs. Brown indicated that Sally should sit down and Sally obediently did so and watched the matron walk around the desk to sit beside her husband. Afterwards, Sally couldn't remember much about the interview; she supposed she told them how much she had always wanted to work with children but it all seemed rather hazy.

After a while, the Browns stood up and Mr. Brown said,

"Well Sally, that all seems fine. We will call your mother in and take you to have your medical. It depends on that now."

This was the bit Sally had been dreading. As she submitted to the examination and answered questions about her health, she worried and prayed, "Please God, let them pass me."

After the examination, Mrs Brown was called in by the doctor. He expressed some concern that Sally would

not be strong enough to do the job. Sally's heart dropped.
They were not going to let her do it! But she had reckoned
without her mother....

"How will you ever know if you don't give her the
chance?"

Emily Brown looked from mother to the daughter,
who was sitting with a pleading expression in her pale
face. She did, indeed, look too delicate to do such a job,
but Emily had listened to everything Sally had said in the
interview and she had taken to her, seeing herself in this
girl; the passion she had for children and the care that she
had in her heart.

"Mrs. Golding, you are so right," Emily said
firmly. "We will give you a month's trial Sally."

"Oh thank you, thank you Mrs Brown! I won't let
you down, I promise!" The smile on the girl's face was a
picture as she at last saw that her dreams just might come
true.

"I will show you both the downstairs of the house,
but I will leave the upstairs for when you join us Sally, as
it's such a large house." Emily Brown led them back into
the large hall. The floor was paved in dull orange and red
tiles, diamond laid, with a boarder. To their right was a
beautiful staircase with shallow stairs and a polished wood
handrail and balustrade. It rose along the wall, with large
windows making it very light. The stair carpet was held in
place with brass stair rods.

"The room you waited in is the Parlour and along
here is the Nursery Family room." They walked passed
another door, which remained shut and went into a room

on the same side of the hall as the Parlour. This was a very large, long room with big windows and French doors giving this room a light and airy feel. There was a large square table nearest the door end surrounded by chairs and at the other end was a piano; in between there was a lot of space, empty except for a couple of armchairs and a carpet square.

They came out of the Nursery and walked towards a corridor opposite the door of the nursery. They went passed a sluice room and a large room with little toilets and hand basins. "For the under-fives to use" explained Mrs. Brown. Then they were in the other corridor, which was much narrower than the entrance hall but was still quite wide, with the same tiled floor. To their left was another staircase.

"These are the stairs we mostly use," said Mrs. Brown, "At one time they would have been the servants' stairs because we are in the kitchen area now."

She walked past the stairs and indicated a room on the same side.

"That is the kitchen. And this," she opened a door opposite the kitchen, "is the Dining Room Family room."

This was a room mostly dominated by the large square table in the centre of the room. In front of the fireplace was a rug flanked by two armchairs. This room had two tall windows, which again ensured that this was a pleasant room, filled with daylight. Sally noticed it faced the front but was at the side. The two hallways formed a 'wrong way round' L, with these rooms in the 'arm' of the L. Emily showed them that there was a storeroom beside the dining room, which at one time had been the Butler's

Pantry. At the end of the corridor was a door, leading straight out onto the pavement.

As Sally walked around the house, she had the uncanny feeling that she had been here before. This was something she had experienced a few times in her life and it told her this was somewhere she was meant to be. This house belonged in her life. But one thing was puzzling her.

"Where are the children?"

Emily laughed. "Well, of course, most of them are at school just now and the little ones have been taken out by the housemothers. We needed a quiet day for interviewing, and as it is a lovely day, they have gone out. I am sure it won't be long before they are back again but you will meet everyone when you join us, and you will have plenty of time to get to know them all."

As she was saying this, Emily was leading Sally and Maureen back towards the large front door.

"You will start on the first of May, Sally. You will need to be here at 7.30 a.m."

They shook hands, and Sally thanked her, then, before they knew it, Sally and her mother were once again standing outside the front door, which was closed again.

Sally threw her arms around her mother's neck and hugged her.

"I did it! I really did it! And it's thanks to you mum too, for saying what you did!"

Maureen hugged her daughter. It was going to be a wrench for her, because Sally would be living in here, but at least she would come home on her days off. They started down the drive, and Sally turned to look at the house just as they passed through the gateway. She couldn't believe her luck.

Chapter 3

Beaumont House

Sally was feeling very nervous now. Jim Golding, Sally's father, was driving her to Beaumont House. It was just after 7a.m., which was quite early for her to be out and about – Sally didn't like mornings very much. But she had to be at the home for 7.30 so an early start was necessary.

As she sat beside her dad, watching the familiar roads, Sally thought about her last weeks at Walkers Nurseries. There she had been a 'jack of all trades'. She had been taken on at the garden centre to type the Boss's letters but as time went on she found herself doing a variety of things: booking orders, answering the phone, keeping the 'Quantities Book', doing the labels for the plants – and was one of only two people who could handle the dreaded duplicating machine! Thus she was able, at a moment's notice, to step into another person's shoes if they were on holiday or off sick. She knew she was like her dad, able to turn her hand to many different things especially when it involved using some kind of machinery. Sally thought sometimes she was just too useful....

Not long after her interview at Beaumont House, Sally was approached by one of the office managers.

"Sally, we would like you to work in the Accounts department for a while."

"Sorry, John, I can't work in Accounts," she replied.

"Why not? You can do everything else. We want you to know how things work in Accounts," explained John.

"Well, for one thing, I'm absolutely useless at maths; I would probably get into an awful mess and bankrupt the business inside a month! But, more importantly, I can't because I'm leaving."

"You're leaving?" John sounded horrified! "Why?"

"Because I have another job, John – one I've always wanted to do – to take care of children in a Home. I shall be starting there at the beginning of May."

John, although startled, congratulated her and said they would miss her. Sally knew she would miss her job here and her daily altercations with the nursery workers that she saw on her walk to and from work. But she was so excited by the prospect of working at Beaumont House that everything paled in comparison. She couldn't wait to get there!

At least, that what she had thought – until now! Now that she was actually on her way, Sally wasn't sure at all – what if she couldn't do the job after all? What if she couldn't control the children? What if......? Her reverie was broken suddenly when her father spoke:

"Here we are!" Sally looked up, startled, and eyed the imposing house as they pulled up on the drive. She climbed out of the car slowly; her heart was beating very fast. Jim hefted her case out of the boot of the car. Nervously, Sally rang the doorbell. In a very short space of time, the door opened and there stood Emily, smiling in welcome.

"Sally – how lovely to see you, we have been looking forward to you coming. Is this your father? Come in/" Emily's smile was so warm that Sally began to relax.

"Yes. This is my dad, Jim Golding. Dad, this is Mrs. Brown, the Matron."

"How do?" Jim shook hands with the matron. She smiled at him, thinking what a nice looking man he was. Sally looked very much like him.

"Would you like to bring Sally's case in for her Mr. Golding? She might be glad for you to take it upstairs for her. We can go up the main stairs as they are easier to climb and will be out of the way of any children coming down."

Sally, despite her nervousness, was thrilled to be able to climb that elegant staircase! She felt like a lady, and for a few moments allowed herself to imagine herself wearing a long beautiful dress....

The staircase only went up one flight. For the next flight up they had to use the other stairs. They were on the top floor of the house and went along a corridor. Matron opened a door and they entered a very large room which contained four single beds with wardrobes and chests of drawers in between them.

"This will be your bed Sally," Matron indicated the bed behind the door. Jim put the case down on the bed. "Don't worry about your things now Sally, you will have time to sort them later. I need to take you down so you can join a family for breakfast."

"I must be getting off, as I should be at work," said Jim. They went back downstairs. There was quite a bit of hustle and bustle around them now as staff and children headed towards the rooms they would be having their breakfast in. They walked to the front door, where Jim kissed his daughter.

"Bye then Topsy," said Jim, "hope you get on well. See you in a few days. Goodbye, Matron, nice to meet you."

"Bye dad."

Matron bade Jim goodbye and shut the door behind him. She turned to Sally.

"Right, Sally; for the first few weeks you will be a 'floater.' This means you will spend a couple of weeks with each family in turn so that you have a chance to get to know all the children. Even though you will ultimately be in one family, it's important that you know all of them as there are times when you will have the others, such as when it's your turn to take them to school or when we are watching them outside. We often have activities all together."

As she was speaking, Emily matron was heading towards the room the Sally's mum had waited in when Sally had her interview, the Parlour. The door was open already.

"I am putting you with Lillian first. She has been here the longest and is my deputy matron. She is lovely and she is the best to help you get to know everything. You will enjoy being with her."

Sally followed Emily into the room, where several children were sitting round the large table, presided over by Aunty Lillian. Next to her was a high chair in which was sat a baby about 10 months old and she was feeding him, spooning his porridge to him. Several pairs of eyes turned enquiringly in Sally's direction.

"Everyone, this is Aunty Sally. She has just joined us; I hope you will all do your best to make her feel at home with us," Emily smiled at them. Lillian looked up and smiled. She was in her late thirties with shoulder-length very dark hair which was naturally wavy. She had warm brown eyes; Sally took to her immediately. A little girl got up from the table and took Sally's hand.

"Come and sit next to me Aunty Sally," she said. Sally smiled at her and sat down at the proffered seat. The little girl was friendly; she told Sally her name was Kate and that she had a sister, whose name was Lucy. She waved her hand at her sister Lucy, who was sitting across the table. Sally looked across at Lucy and saw a slightly older girl than Kate; they looked similar in some ways, although Lucy was wearing glasses. Lucy smiled shyly at Sally.

There were about nine children of assorted ages round the table and the baby in the high chair. There was a very friendly atmosphere as the children interacted with Aunty Lillian and with each other, not loudly, but definitely not subdued either. Sally concentrated on trying to note the children's names and listening to their chatter as she ate her own breakfast. This was a happy 'family.'

The day passed quickly as Aunty Lillian guided her around the required jobs. The aunties, after seeing the older children off to school, made the beds and swept the floors of the bedrooms and the family rooms, sorted the clean clothes into all the right children's drawers and anything else that needed doing. Whilst this was happening, other staff looked after the small, preschool children, who would all play together in the nursery, or sometimes a housemother would decide to take 'their' children out, either to a park or downtown, or just out for a walk. All sorts of things went on during the day; sometimes the children were just taken outside to play in the garden, sometimes they were allowed in the 'playroom', which was a special room next to the nursery which was normally kept locked. This room had all sorts of larger toys in it, such as a rocking horse and a dolls' house and so on.

As time went on, Sally grew to really love the house; she'd always had a vivid imagination and could really 'see' the house as it had been in more genteel days, when it had a family and servants running it. The playroom was a favourite of hers as she could see, above the very large cupboards that the room still had its original decorative features on the ceiling and this room also had large windows with patio doors, although these were never opened. This was a perfect house in many ways for a children's home; it was a tough, resilient house with plenty of space. At the same time, it managed to be homely.

The gardens were watched over by Uncle Walter. Although the children were allowed to play on the sweeping lawns and the hard area around the house, woe betide any child who dared go near his greenhouse! Of course, there were children who would dare – Kate was one of them – she was quite a lively child, Sally found! Kate told her once that she had been at Beaumont House 'forever'. Lillian told Sally this was indeed the case, as Kate was only about 18 months old when she came into care; she was now six.

Sally had always imagined that children in a children's' home would be mostly orphans; however, this was not the case. There was, in fact, only one child out of the thirty-odd children in the home who was actually an orphan; that was the baby in Lillian's family. All the others had parents; at least one and often two, but for some reason or another they were not able to look after their children so they were in care. Some had been placed there by their parents; others had been taken by the local authority.

The routines of the house were soon very familiar to Sally as the days went by. She was getting to know the children and the other members of staff. She shared a bedroom with the three other nursery assistants, Andrea, Susan and Jane. The girls got along well with each other. Susan was the youngest, having started work there at the age of sixteen for work experience. She was the nursery assistant in the Nursery family; Andrea worked with Lillian and Jane was nursery assistant to Marjorie. Sally didn't know Marjorie yet; she was due to have her stint in the Dining Room Family whilst Jane was having her holiday in a couple of weeks. The other housemother was Valerie, in the Nursery Family. Sally had her two weeks in the Parlour Family with Lillian whilst Andrea was away, so Sally had not yet met her either. When Andrea came back, Sally would move into the Nursery Family whilst Susan had her holiday.

The fortnight in the Nursery family was ok; Sally didn't like Valerie as much as Lillian; she was younger and very strict. There were a few more children in the Nursery family than there were in the Parlour, including a family of four children, three girls and a boy who were very much alike. The Nursery family bedroom was a large one where most of the children slept; in fact all the families had one large bedroom each but there were some smaller rooms where just a couple of children slept, usually related to each other. There was one bedroom where two sisters slept and another where two little brothers slept. And yet another that was shared by two older girls.

Sally was fairly relieved when the time came to move on to the Dining room family; although she loved the children, she didn't get on terribly well with Valerie. She was told that the Dining room family was in fact the largest family, with thirteen children. She had already met most of the children in the four weeks she had been there. As she looked round at the children seated around the table at their tea, her eyes stopped at two little boys, whom she knew to be brothers, Davey and John Adams. Davey looked back at her and their eyes met. Somehow, in that moment, Sally knew that there was something about him, that he was going to be special to her. It was only a momentary thing and it passed quickly as the business of dishing out food and eating and talking around the table ensued. Marjorie was off duty that day and the table was presided over by Jane, the other Nursery Assistant. It was a happy meal and Sally knew this was where she wanted to be – if only.... but she also knew this wasn't likely just now, that she was going to remain a 'floater', covering for whoever was having their days off. But at least she could enjoy her fortnight with this family before she started doing cover.

This was her family; she just knew it. As she got to know the three little sisters, the children of a mother who kept having babies by different fathers and then putting them into care, the two sisters; so not alike; the younger one with big eyes and curly hair and who never stopped talking and her older, quieter sister who had dark straight hair. There were another two sisters, very close in age; one eight, the other nine. The younger one had lovely curly hair; the other had blond hair too but was only mildly wavy. There were two sisters who were in their early teens; one dark, the other blond who shared a two-bed room, Davey and John who shared a room, and then there was the 'baby of the family', a little boy of about three who had a cheeky smile; she grew to love them all so much.

Marjorie was back the next morning after Sally's first tea with the Dining room family. Jane had departed for her holiday when she left duty that night. As the housemothers had their own rooms upstairs, Sally didn't meet Marjorie until that breakfast time. She wasn't sure what to think of her; there was nothing she could put her finger on exactly, something just didn't feel quite right about her. Marjorie was very attractive, with blond hair curling at her neck and a slim figure. She seemed very pleasant, but her smile didn't quite reach her eyes. The children reacted differently to her, Sally noticed. When Jane was with them, they were happy and laughing but with Marjorie there they were quieter and just took their food and ate. And when the meal was done, they got up and went upstairs to get ready for school without being told.

Sally got on with the daily routine because she was familiar with it now. Marjorie told her a bit about the children as they worked together. Things seemed ok. Later in the day, when the older children were in school, Marjorie decided they would take their small children, of which they had five, for a walk into town. They would take a pushchair each and they would take it in turns to give the children rides; the two youngest would ride the most. It worked well and they enjoyed their outing; however, Sally noticed that sometimes Marjorie was very sharp with the children and the ones with her were very quiet. The children with Sally were laughing and pointing at things and she was talking with them as they walked along. They went into a cafe and bought them all drinks so they could rest a while before they started on the walk back up the hill to Beaumont House. It was dinner time when they got back. Sally was doing a split shift that day; she was having the afternoon off then coming back on at four and working until eight o'clock. Lillian was on the two until ten shift. It was the job of the two women on the late shift to look after the children in bed until the night nurse came on.

As Sally was patrolling the corridors at bedtime, she happened to look into Davey and John's bedroom. She was just in time to see John doing something in the corner of the room. She stopped, wondering what he was doing. As she watched, she saw something wet spreading across the floor and she realised what John was doing. John turned round then and saw her. He stopped, looking at her, unsure.

"What's this John?" Sally asked quietly. "Why are you doing that?"

John stood silently before her, head down, gazing at the floor.

"Well?" Sally was still quiet. "I'm waiting. The bathroom is only just down the corridor. Were you that desperate that you couldn't wait?"

John looked up at her then, eyes defiant.

Sally could see she wasn't going to get anything out of him, so she sent him off to clean his teeth, sighed and went to fetch the mop and bucket. Then she carried on checking the children and soon forgot about the incident.

A week or so later, she was on the two until ten shift, with Marjorie on the split shift. She was in one of the children's rooms, putting one of the little ones back into bed after she had climbed out of her cot for the third time when she heard Marjorie's voice raised down the landing. Tentatively, she went to see what was going on. She knew she had to tread warily with Marjorie...

When she got to Davey and John's bedroom, she was shocked to see Marjorie hitting Davey and shouting at him.

"You've done it again, you filthy little boy!" Davey was standing in front of her, crying. Sally's eyes went to the corner of the room. There was the tell-tale puddle...

"Oh, Aunty Marjorie!" Sally blurted out, before she realised what she was doing. Marjorie turned to look at her.

"Don't interfere, Sally!" she said furiously. "I'm sorting this out. Davey has to learn he can't do things like this. You go back to what you were doing."

"Davey didn't do it!" Sally stood firm. Marjorie looked at her disbelieving. "How do you know? You weren't here!"

"No, I wasn't this time, but I caught John doing it a few days ago! I saw him doing it – and I cleaned it up that time! It's John doing this, not Davey!"

Marjorie looked at Sally and searched her face; she could see she was speaking the truth. Then she looked at Davey who looked back at her steadily. Then she turned round and walked out of the room. Davey and Sally looked at each other and then she put her arm around his shoulders. He put his arms around her slim waist and cuddled her.

"Thank you, Aunty Sally,"

"Has this happened to you a lot Davey?" Sally asked softly.

"Yes, Aunty, it's happened a lot and Aunty Marjorie always hits me for it. John does it on purpose but I couldn't tell anyone that he does it."

"Why not?"

"Because my dad made me promise to look after John and that means not letting him get into trouble. But sometimes I think he does it on purpose to get me into trouble. I don't know why 'cos I've always tried to look after him."

"Sometimes children do things but they don't really understand why they do them, Davey. Perhaps it's got something to do with being here. He needs to learn that it is very wrong to get you into trouble but don't worry; you won't get blamed for that anymore."

"There will be something else. He will think of something. And Aunty Marjorie hates me."

"Oh Davey! I'm sure that's not true; she doesn't hate you. How could she hate a lovely boy like you?" Sally held him away from her then so she could look at his face and smile at him. He smiled back at her. From that moment on, Sally knew her heart was lost and Davey, for his part, became her willing slave! Not that she took advantage of that; he never got any more jobs than the other children did, but he loved it when she was around. He missed her when she was working in another family.

Also from that moment, Sally took to watching the Davey/Aunt Marjorie situation carefully. She could see that Davey was indeed right, he did get blamed for things that he didn't do; Marjorie did seem to thoroughly dislike him. Sally wondered what she could do about it.

Sally also began to wonder if she could do something about Marjorie herself; she never seemed very happy. Was there some reason why she was like that?

Chapter 4

Plans

Sally decided that her first move had to be to talk with Emily matron. This she did one day when she knew that Marjorie was on her days off and was not around. They went to talk in Emily's office. Emily was curious as to why Sally had asked if they could have a talk.

"Come in Sally. What's the problem? You are happy working with us?" she enquired worriedly.

"Oh yes! I love it! It's everything I hoped it would be," Sally smiled as she sat down. "There is something that's bothering me quite a lot. It's difficult though."

"Just say it dear!" Emily was encouraging.

"Well, it's Marjorie," Sally noted Emily's expression; half quizzical, but she sort of nodded as if she wasn't surprised. "I don't want to speak out of turn...."

"Don't worry dear; I don't suppose you can say anything that I don't already know about!"

"I suppose so. Oh, matron! I am so worried by the way she treats Davey!" Sally blurted it out all at once. "I have stopped her blaming him for wetting in the corner of their room but –"

"You have?" interrupted Emily, "How did you do that?"

"I happened to see John doing it one evening. So, when it happened again and Marjorie was punishing Davey for it, I went and told her that I had seen John doing it."

Emily raised her eyebrows. "That was brave of you. I bet Marjorie didn't like that."

"No, she didn't but she had to listen because she could see I was speaking the truth. I have been watching her since then and there is no doubt she targets Davey. He is always getting into trouble with her for something. And she hits him so hard sometimes, it worries me so much."

"Yes, it's been worrying me and I have had words with her. She was better for a while but it seems to have started again doesn't it?"

"Oh yes it has. And he is really a lovely boy; I don't know why she has taken against him like that."

"Nor do I, dear," sighed Emily. "If she doesn't change, I'm going to have to let her go."

Sally looked at her sadly. She didn't want to see Marjorie being sacked.

"Isn't there anything that can be done? You know, Marjorie never seems to be happy, does she? The other girls don't like her very much."

"They don't. But there must be a reason why she is like that. It's been puzzling me a lot since I came here, wondering if anything can be done."

"I have an idea or two," said Sally, "but I will need your permission to start working on my ideas."

"Well, that's encouraging; I'm sure I will be happy to go along with any ideas you might have to make things better."

When Sally walked out of Emily's office, both the young woman and the older woman were feeling very hopeful. Sally decided to start putting things into action that very evening.

Sally began to form the habit of coming to see Davey at the end of each of her working days, even when she had been working in another family. In order to not make it too obvious, she would do the rounds of all the children before she went off duty and paid others lots of attention and gave out cuddles where needed. They all loved her and looked forward to their nightly cuddles and kisses from her. Davey loved the goodnight times, especially when he had been in trouble, he knew she would make him feel better. Then, one night, she took the plan further.

"Right then; I've decided I'm going to read you a story," said Sally, after seeing that Davey and John were ready for bed. "What would you like me to read? John, pop downstairs and get a book."

John sped off from the bedroom and Sally talked quietly with Davey until John came back, holding his favourite story book. They settled down on Davey's bed, which was the one just inside the door and Sally began to read. Other children from the bedrooms either side heard her reading and crept in to listen. Before long, the bed held as many children as could get on it and yet more sat on John's bed and others squatted on the floor in front of Sally.

After that, Sally would often read a story to the children in Davey's room, children from other rooms crowding in to sit on the two boys' beds. Davey would sit on one side of her and John often on the other side. She made sure she gave him fuss too and sometimes sat with her arm around him, whilst Davey leaned against her other side. The children would kneel or sit behind her, craning their necks to see the pictures as she read. Of course, it would depend on who was on late duty - if Marjorie or Valerie were on, Sally didn't do it. She just said her goodnights and went upstairs. Lillian, Jane, Andrea and Susan didn't mind if she read a story, provided she made sure all the children went back to bed afterwards, which they did because she said if they didn't, they wouldn't be able to come to the next story telling session!

It wasn't long before the other Aunties started doing the same thing; after their duty hours were over they would come and see the children and kiss them goodnight and read to them. Sally was glad because it was impossible to get thirty children into Davey's bedroom to read to them – and they had all wanted to come! Now, there would be more than one story telling session going on at the same time, sometimes three, depending on who had the time to do it. And it went on when Sally wasn't there, which took some of the focus off the fact that really she was doing it for Davey.... Even Valerie and Marjorie started doing it! They didn't do it as often as the others but at least they did it. If Sally was around and Marjorie wanted to tell the story, Sally would sit and cuddle two children whilst they listened....

These sessions didn't happen every night because the Aunties didn't always have the time, but they were greatly looked forward to by the children and Aunties alike.

Sally was pleased that this idea had taken off in such a big way. Now she had to work on the next part of her plan.

On Friday and Saturday evenings the girls who were in the house but off duty would go to a dance, either at The Hostel in Hereford, or at Wormelow, which was a village a few miles out of Hereford that had a great dance hall. Often groups would play at these places and it was exciting to see a famous group. They enjoyed the dances that included some ballroom dancing too. Sally loved the social life she had at Beaumont House and enjoyed the boys she met at the dances!

She noticed that Marjorie hardly ever went out with them; the girls simply didn't ask her.

"I think we should ask Marjorie to come with us when we go to dances," she said to Jane, Susan and Andrea one evening when they were changing in their bedroom after work one evening.

"You must be joking!" Susan exclaimed, "Whatever for? She doesn't like us and we certainly don't like her!"

"It's just that I think if we included her, get friendlier with her, she might become a bit nicer. I'm bothered about how she treats Davey and if she gets happier, she might be kinder to him."

The others nodded slowly, understanding where Sally was coming from.

"Well, she is obviously not a very happy person; perhaps it would help her be better if we took her out with us," agreed Andrea. "What does Lillian think about it?"

Lillian was surprised to see the four nursery assistants come to her bedroom. She invited them in and they put Sally's idea to her and explaining why they felt they should include Marjorie. Lillian was all for it; she agreed it might help a better working relationship between them all if Marjorie felt they were her friends.

The next Friday night when they were all going out, she knocked on Marjorie's bedroom door. When Marjorie opened it, Sally said,

"Why aren't you ready yet, Marj? We are going to miss the bus to Wormelow if we don't get going soon."

"But I'm not coming."

"Why aren't you coming? We all go, don't we? Come on, get your glad-rags on quickly and fix your make-up; you'll enjoy it."

So Marjorie chose a dress to wear and quickly did her hair and make-up. She couldn't help feeling a bit excited; she had never been out with the girls before but Sally seemed to want her to go with them.

When she came out of her room, she looked stunning.

"Wow Marjorie, you look amazing. You've got such a great figure, you should wear a dress more often. Are we all ready, girls? Let's go!"

So saying, they made their way carefully down the stairs and out of the house, laughing and joking as they walked down the road to the bus station where they were catching the bus. The other girls agreed that Marjorie looked great and it was a very happy bunch of girls who got on the bus. They got many admiring looks and a few wolf-whistles from some lads on the bus. Marjorie was happy; this was going to be fun!

They did indeed have a great time and after that Sally made sure Marjorie went out with them if she was free and gradually Marjorie started softening a bit and joining in with them. She didn't find it easy, that was obvious, because she hadn't been included before. But Sally pretended not to notice. She always complimented Marjorie on her hair or the way she looked once ready to go out, and would link arms with her as they walked to the bus stop. One day she was going to get friendly enough to try to get to the bottom of some things. In the meantime, her campaign to try to get Marjorie to feel more part of them was working.

Valerie was the only one who wasn't part of the plan; she had a fiancé and hardly ever went out with the others anyway. In any case, she was only concerned with her own family and rarely saw what Marjorie was like with Davey.

Lillian, although quite a bit older than the others, was very much part of them, and, as deputy matron, she was also very concerned about the Marjorie/Davey situation. She had a kind heart and agreed that Marjorie should be included in their outings; she had realised that this was not a happy girl. So, although not all of them could go out at once, because there had to be two staff in the house in the evenings and there was always someone having their days off, those who remained when the dances were on went together. They decided between them where they would go, depending on what groups were playing. Wormelow was very much the favourite of the girls; the only problem was that, although they could get a bus out there, they would have to get a taxi back, which they shared. Although sometimes one girl would manage to pick up a boy with a car and twist his arm to take all of them home!

Over time, Sally 'picked up' quite a few really nice lads and a few not so nice, who she never saw again. She rarely went out with any boys she met at a dance, although there was one who turned out to have grown up in a children's home in Kent. He was in the area working with the natural gas team, as this was the time when natural gas, recently discovered in the North Sea, was being brought all over the country. He was part of the gang laying the pipes. He was in the area for a few weeks. Sally didn't really fancy him all that much, but he really liked her and so her kind heart meant she saw him a few times when he was in the area. When he moved on with his gang, he tried to keep in touch with her but in the end Sally had to tell him that she didn't really want to keep in contact anymore. She felt very bad about it, but, as the others said to her, if there is no chance she was going to fall for him, it was better to tell him straight away.

Sally had never had a social life like this; wonderful dances to go to and friends to go with; before she had lived in Hereford, she was very much a loner, very shy. Her year working at Walker's Nurseries had brought her more out of herself as everyone was so friendly, but even then she only occasionally had friends to go out with. So she was really enjoying this. Not only did she have her dream job but she had so much more; friendship, fun and loads of children to love – not to mention the freedom which could only come from not living at home! Although she still loved going home on her days off.

When she was at home one day, she said to her mother:

"Mum, how would you feel if I bring a child home with me sometimes?"

"I don't mind at all love, provided you look after them," was the reply. Sally knew that Jane and Andrea took children to their homes sometimes so she decided to start bringing Davey and other children home with her on her days off.

Davey absolutely loved the times he spent at Sally's home with her and her parents. Her dad Jim soon became Granddad Jim and eventually her mum became Granny Mo. In fact, Davey adored Granddad Jim, he loved to spend time with him watching him work in his shed doing all kinds of things and on work days he even went to watch him at work in the workshop belonging to Walker's Nursery.

The farmhouse they lived in was in the middle of a country lane but was surrounded by nursery land and to get to Granddad Jim's workshop they only had to go across the garden and through a gateway. He loved the smell of the petrol and oil and adored watching Granddad at work, fixing the vehicles belonging to the nursery. It could be anything from tractors to lorries; Granddad Jim could fix anything - he was Davey's hero! When he grew up, Davey wanted to be a mechanic just like granddad Jim – in fact, he wanted to work here with him! It was his dream – to always be part of this family and to work with his hero. Jim always made the lad feel useful, getting him to hand him tools, sending him on small errands around the nursery. The nursery workers got used to seeing him around and would greet him cheerfully. However, Davey could only be here on workdays during the school holidays.

Maureen was indulgent to the boy too; she always made sure she had the things he loved to eat when he came. She knew she spoiled Davey but she loved him very much and she missed seeing her grandsons who still lived in Norfolk.

Best of all, Davey loved it when he could stay there for a couple of nights when Sally had her long weekend. She and Jim would come to fetch him on Friday evenings after school and he would stay Saturday and Sunday with them. Granddad Jim worked on Saturday mornings, so Davey would spend time there with him, popping to and from the farmhouse when he liked. In the afternoon, they would go shopping. Davey enjoyed being in the town with them, walking so proudly, pretending they were his family and it was the most natural thing in the world to be out shopping with them!

Granny Mo always bought 'special bread' on Saturdays, crispy rolls for Saturday and a cottage loaf for Sunday tea. He loved the cottage loaves – they had big round bottoms and a smaller round top, rather like a bread snowman. The top had a thumb-sized dent in it where the baker had pushed the dough down with his thumb to make sure the two pieces stuck together. Davey and Granddad Jim always argued for the top slice of the upper piece which was golden brown and crispy! They usually ended up cutting it in half and sharing it! Then there was the 'bloomers' and other kinds of long rolls, when Davey and Granddad Jim each had to have the 'knobbledy' off the ends! Sally remembered the times when she and her sister used to vie with their dad for the coveted pieces of bread –

and indeed, she still did when Davey wasn't there! But she always kept quiet and let him have his fun with her father, laughing at their antics.

Then there was the wrestling to watch on television, with Jackie Pallo, Mick McManus, Adrian Street, Giant Haystacks and others. They would get so excited, jumping up and down in their seats and shouting at the television! Then perhaps in the evening there would be a good Western to watch –'Hoss Muck and Gunpowder' as Granddad Jim would call them! Maureen would watch her husband indulgently; they had never had sons and Jim so loved having a boy around! Although she knew that Sally and her dad had always been best buddies and Sally had stuck to her dad like glue when she was young, just as Davey was doing now.

On summer evenings they would play in the garden, chasing each other around in mad games or pretend wrestling; there was so much ground – there were two large ponds with a spinney of trees in between them and a large lawn that had to be mowed by a ride-on mower, usually done by someone from the nursery. Often they would picnic on the lawn, watching the moorhens on the ponds. Sometimes Sally would get out her guitar and sing to them. It was very peaceful as the nearest neighbours were right down the end of the lane; Sally felt ok singing when there was no one else but her family to hear! And she had a beautiful voice, so clear and tuneful; Davey loved to hear her. She could play the piano too and on days when it was too wet or cold to be outside, she sometimes played to them and sung to the piano instead of her guitar. In Davey's eyes she could do no wrong; whatever she did was just fine by him! He was seeing her in her natural environment; he learned to separate that from the role she played at Beaumont House, where she had to be quite strict and had to look after all the other children.

There were times when she took another child home, which he really hated but understood.

"You see Davey, the other children need to feel they are wanted and loved too," Sally had explained to him seriously one evening when she had told him she was going to take Michelle home with her the next day. "Sometimes I must take someone else home with me. But you will come with me the most and you will be the only one who will stay with us overnight. The others will only be with me for the day and they will be brought back after tea." She hugged him, and he held her tight.

"All right Aunty, I will try not to mind," he said, looking at her seriously with his big brown eyes. Sally felt her heart turn over, as it always did when he looked at her like that.

Sally had had to get special permission from matron to have Davey stay at her house overnight; normally it wasn't done. But Emily felt this was something that Davey needed – to get away from Marjorie sometimes, to have his own space and to be freed for a while from the worry of always having to look after John – and often being blamed for his misdemeanours. Of course, John was clever; he behaved immaculately when Davey wasn't there to get blamed for what he did! There was no doubt that this attention was doing the boy good; he was so much happier these days – even Margery seemed to have lightened up on him. Emily just blessed the day when she took on Sally; the girl had brought a special kind of sunshine to Beaumont House.

Chapter 5

How Time Flies

Sally's first year at Beaumont House absolutely flew by. It seemed there was always something going on.

Of course at first came her weeks of settling in and learning about the children and the staff, which really took her very little time; she was soon well into everyone!

It was the practise of the home to take the children on a two week holiday at the seaside during the summer. During this time, two of the Aunties would stay behind to supervise the spring cleaning of the house with the domestic staff. It was decided the first summer that Sally would stay behind with Lillian.

It was odd at the house without the children and cleaning the house was a lot of work, but Sally enjoyed it immensely. She and Lillian got on really well with each other and with the cleaning staff, Auntie Agnes and Auntie Sylvia. Together they scrubbed walls and everything that needed cleaning and there was a lot of laughing and joking going on. The two cleaning ladies were great fun and they all worked so well together. It was a very large house to clean but they did it methodically and easily got it done before the children came home again.

Of course, they only cleaned the house during working hours and then Lillian and Sally enjoyed quiet evenings together watching television and chatting. They ate their meals together in the dining room with Agnes and Sylvia during the day and in the evenings it was just the two of them. It wasn't possible to have their days off whilst the children were away because there had to be two staff at the house in case a child needed to be brought in, but that first year, all was quiet.

The children came home after the fortnight, full of stories about the wonderful time they'd had at the seaside. Lillian and Sally were very glad to see them back. Sally wondered how things had been for Davey, but he had been with Aunty Jane, so all was well. However, that bedtime, Davey put his arms around Sally's neck when she kissed him goodnight.

"I enjoyed the holiday, Aunty Sally, but I did miss you," he whispered.

"I missed you too, but I'm glad you had a good time. It has been very quiet here without you all; I'm happy to have you all back home again."

As November drew near, Marjorie was talking with Sally.

"We have a lovely time on Bonfire Night, Sally. The fire service always sends us a fire engine and men and they put on a lovely firework display for us and a bonfire outside. We all go into the Nursery and watch through the big French windows."

And indeed, she was right. The children were very excited to have the men there and they all waited expectantly by the Nursery windows. They were not disappointed, for the bonfire was great and they ooh-d and ahh-d at the fireworks. When the display was over, the French doors were opened and the children were allowed to have a sparkler each but they had to be outside and individually watched over by an adult. Then they came back in for toffee apples and other goodies all provided by the firemen, who had brought everything with them.

"We always look forward to our evening up here with the kids," The engine chief told Sally. "It is fun and shows that Bonfire Night can be enjoyed without it being dangerous."

Sally nodded. "Yes. I've never really liked fireworks; my sister and I had a few nasty experiences when we were young because boys used to chase us with Jumping Jacks. I've been afraid of them ever since."

She looked around her in the large room at all the children and adults there.

"It really is good to see them having such a good time. We are so grateful to all you men for coming to do this. I have really enjoyed it myself."

"It's a pleasure, young miss." At that moment, his radio at his waist bleeped. He took it out and answered, "Yes?" He listened for a moment and then, "we'll be there right away."

He went over to Emily and said, "I'm sorry ma'am, we have to answer a call. We need to go right away. The fire is almost out now; perhaps your gardener will see that it is out properly but we will come back to check it after this job." He raised his voice, "Sorry kids, we have to go as we have a call. Enjoy the rest of your evening."

At that, he strode out of the French doors, followed swiftly by his men and, moments later, the children crowded to the window once again to watch the engine as it left the grounds, blue lights flashing. Once out of the gateway, the bell was sounding as they sped away into the night. Sally murmured a prayer to keep them safe and then went to join a group of her children.

****

"Don't forget to save your stockings, Sally," Jane said to her one day, soon after Bonfire Night.

"Save my stockings?" Sally was puzzled. "What for?"

"All us aunties do a stocking each for the children; we save our laddered stockings so we can use them. We buy little things like pencils, rulers, rubbers, colouring books, crayons, sweets and so on for the children in our families. Perhaps you would like to come in with Marjorie and me as we have the largest family?"

"Oh yes, I'll so that. I already have a few stockings that are no good to wear anymore."

"That's great. We will get together and decided how we will do it."

Sally was excited at the thought of being able to do stockings for the children; she remembered all the wonderful stockings she'd had growing up and the Christmas mornings when she and her sister would open their stockings in bed, sitting in one bed together, comparing what they had; often they had the same things in different colours or designs. And then they packed all the gifts up and get into bed with mum to show her what they had got! Sally had loved that time the best; to this day she remembered some of the little novelty things she had found in her stocking over the years.

Preparations for Christmas were soon upon them; each child was to be given a gift paid for by the local authority and the staff had the job of going to Chadds, the famous department store of Hereford, to choose the gifts. Sally enjoyed that very much as she went with Marjorie, Jane being on her days off at the time. Marjorie had a list of what all the children in her family had asked for and they went round the toy department selecting the right things. The toys were left at the store to be delivered to the home at a later date.

Sally was on rota to be on her days off on Christmas Day, but she elected to stay at Beaumont House for the morning so she could be there when the children opened their presents. The pleasure on their faces when they saw what they had was pure joy for the Aunties who loved these children so much. Sally thought about all the gifts she had always received at Christmas from her parents and other relations. These children only had one gift each, and yet they never moaned or complained; they were so happy. Later there would be Christmas Dinner and in the afternoon there would be games and other fun, followed by 'party' teas. But Sally was going home to have dinner with her mum and dad and spend the rest of Christmas with them. Jim came to pick her up about twelve and there was much hugging and kissing before she went off with her dad.

Sally always loved Christmas at home but this year of course she had missed some of it with being at Beaumont House. Her parents had been to church without her for the Christmas Carol service. But she was here now; and it had always been tradition in her family to 'do' presents in the afternoon, so they still had that to come. As Sally opened her presents she told her parents all about the children and the gifts they had received and all the joy they had experienced as they had opened their one gift. And about what would be happening during the afternoon to make it special for them. Jim and Maureen listened to Sally intently; they always loved to hear about the children and the things they did at the home. It made all of them so thankful for what they had in their lives.

****

One day, very soon after Christmas, Sally was on the two until ten shift. She didn't feel very well and had stayed in bed as long as possible before she had to go on duty. She somehow got through the afternoon but in the early evening she was so very cold and went into the kitchen to 'hug' the Aga, which was always on. She had to get the staff supper ready.....

Emily Matron walked in and took one look at her and ordered her to bed!

"Oh, but Aunty Emily, I can't go to bed; I'm on until ten."

"That doesn't matter. You're ill. Go to bed at once. Don't worry about your duty, someone else will do it."

So Sally went to bed, very thankfully.

For the next few days, she barely moved from her bed and hardly knew anything as her temperature raged. She had flu; if she could have thought much at the time she would have thought that she had never felt so ill in her life.

Emily matron looked after her, sponging her down every few hours. The hours passed unnoticed; when she had to visit the bathroom she was too weak to go unaided. After a week, matron deemed that she was 'well' enough to be taken home, so Jim came to fetch her. She went straight to bed at home and stayed there a further two weeks. After that, she started getting up a little each day, but still spending much of her time in bed. Sally ended up having six weeks off work and was very bored by the time she was well enough to go back to work.

On the day Sally returned to Beaumont House, she was greeted joyfully by the children, who were all very glad to see her back. Many of them came and hugged her and she smiled down at their little faces, so happy to see them all again. Davey waited until the others had finished, then shyly put his arms around her.

"Hello Aunty," he said, his voice muffled in her clothes and he hugged her as tight as he could. She sat down on a nearby chair and drew him onto her lap.

"Hello Davey love. I've missed you very much," she looked up at the others "I have missed you all."

"Are you all better Aunty?" asked Davey, "We have waited for you to come back to us; we have all missed you a lot."

"Yes, I am better now, thank you, dear."

"You must have been very poorly 'cos you have been away ever so long."

"Yes, I was very poorly and I was still very weak after I started to get better which is why I have been away so long."

"I was afraid you weren't coming back," Sally looked into Davey's face and saw all sorts of things revealed in his expression. She hugged him closer and said quietly in his ear, "has it been bad love?"

"Quite bad," he nodded, "but it's better now you are here again."

Sally's heart beat painfully in her chest when she realised what this little boy had probably been through while she had been away; getting into trouble and on top of that, being afraid she wasn't coming back. She felt tears prickle her eyes and she bowed her head in order to hide any tears from the children. When she knew they were under control again, she lifted her head and said brightly.

"Well, I'm back now! Shall I come to read to you tonight?" She saw lots of nods and smiles around her. "Whose turn is it to choose a story I wonder? I have lost track with me being away for so long! Right now, you all need to get hands washed because tea will be put on the table in a few minutes."

Sally got up, putting Davey back on his feet and the children dispersed to wash their hands in readiness for tea. Sally wasn't on duty until the next day, but she was going to eat with the family.

Marjorie was on her days off, so it was Jane in charge and they had a happy meal together as they told her about little things that had been happening whilst she had been off sick.

Life at Beaumont House resumed as normal for Sally and the children and Sally also renewed her efforts to befriend and soften Marjorie. In March, Jane left

Beaumont House to get married and so Sally was moved into the dining room family as the permanent nursery assistant to Marjorie.

Easter came and that meant more fun and games for the children with egg hunts and other games outside as the weather was very mild for the time of year. April also brought Sally's nineteenth birthday and, as she was at work for that day, the cook made her a cake and she shared her birthday tea with the dining room family. Then she went home for the evening to celebrate with her parents.

During the first week of May, a fair would fill the streets of Hereford town centre for three days; obviously known as the Mayfair. Sally was on her days off during this time and because it was a school week, she took no children home with her. The Mayfair was always held on the Tuesday, Wednesday and Thursday of the first week. When Sally returned to work on the Thursday of that week, she learned that the children had been taken down to the fair the day before. They had each been allowed enough money for a ride and a go on a sideshow, or to buy a sweet treat such as a 'dummy' or candy-floss. Davey came to her and put something in her hand.

"Aunty Sally, I tried to win something special by hooking a duck. I didn't win anything but the man let me choose something small. I want to give it to you because I love you."

Sally looked at what he had given her; it was a key-ring with a tiger hanging on it. It was a plastic tiger with a sort of flock coating, which made it look furry. She was touched that he had given it to her. He never had anything and he had spent his sixpence on a sideshow and given her his prize! She felt a lump in her throat as she looked down at his face as he waited anxiously to see if she liked it.

"Oh Davey, it's lovely! Are you sure you want to give it to me? Don't you want to keep it yourself?"

"No Aunty, I choose him because I thought you would like him and I wanted to give you something."

"Thank you sweetheart; I will always treasure it," she bent down and kissed him on his cheek. He went bright red and she laughed and hugged him. She put it in her pocket and got on then with her work. But later, when she went up to her room, she put Davey's sixpenny tiger on her dressing table so she could see it every day.

****

That summer, Sally went with the children on the seaside holiday. They went to West Wales, at a holiday village called Gilfach-y-halen. The children were very excited on the coach going across Wales to the coast; it was quite a noisy journey! As they drew near to the holiday village, they all peered out of the windows eagerly to see what it was like and it was a charming place. Near the entrance was a reception building and next to it a pub, which they called the club, which had an 'olde' worlde' look about it; it certainly wasn't a new building. The road wound downhill and either side of the road were small 'chalets'; they were going to have several of them with a housemother and a few children in each. Some of them had a lovely view overlooking the grassy areas above the beach and there was another winding road that led down to the private beach cove. It was a beautiful setting.

Sally had Davey, John, two sisters, Alice and Marie, and an older girl, Belinda in her chalet. Next door, Andrea had her little group. They couldn't wait to get down to see the beach and before long, all the children and aunties were down there, even though there was not much day left.

The holiday went well; most of the time they spent on the beach because the weather was superb. One day they took the children into Abergavenny. Sometimes in the evenings the aunties went to the clubhouse to have a drink and a chat while one of them would patrol the chalets to make sure all the children were safe in their beds. Other evenings, they gathered outside one of the chalets to drink hot chocolate and enjoy the evening sunshine.

There were stables on the complex too and one day the groom and his stable staff took everyone for a sedate walk around the holiday village on the horses; they took it in turns. Sally wasn't at all sure that riding was something that came naturally to her and was very glad that the groom was walking beside the horse, controlling it and all she had to do was hang on! She was quite glad when she could dismount so that someone else could have a turn.

All in all, it was a very enjoyable holiday, especially as it was Marjorie's turn to stay behind with Susan to do the spring cleaning.

They returned to Beaumont House and prepared for the return to school. Sally couldn't believe that the year had passed so fast.

Chapter 6

A Pivotal Moment

"Gizza chip!"

Sally looked up from the bench where she was sitting with Andrea, eating the chips they had just bought from the chip shop nearby. She saw a pair of smiling blue eyes, a face with dimpled cheeks and a head of beautiful dark wavy hair. Inwardly, she thought: 'Mmmm, *very* nice!' She held up her bag of chips towards him. He reached out and took one, popping it into his mouth and ate slowly, gazing at her all the time. When he finished, he said,

"Thanks! I'm Joe, and this is my mate Pete," he indicated to his mate hovering just behind him. Pete was obviously older than Joe. He was not attractive like Joe was, but he had a nice face, the kind of face you would trust. Andrea moved along so the pair of them could sit down. Sally was so drawn towards Joe; she couldn't take her eyes off him, he was so beautiful! It was obvious that Joe was very taken with her. He included Andrea and Pete in the conversation they were having, but it was so apparent he was only interested in Sally. Andrea watched with amused eyes as the two of them talked; they looked so good together. She turned her attention to Pete and the two of them sat and chatted quietly, letting the other two have a space of sorts. The two girls continued to share their chips with the lads.

"Can I take you out sometime?" asked Joe hopefully. Sally was pleased and she nodded her consent.

Joe was not going to let the grass grow under his feet with this girl! "Tomorrow night?" he asked.

Sally said that would be just fine and he arranged to pick her up from Beaumont House at 7.30 the next evening.

Joe and Pete walked the two girls back to Beaumont House and they stood talking outside the door for quite a while, until, reluctantly, they turned to go in.

"Until tomorrow evening then," said Joe and he touched Sally's hand briefly as he turned to go. She nodded, smiling. Then she was gone.

Pete and Joe turned to each other as they walked across the road.

"You've turned up trumps there mate!" said Pete.

"Yes matey; I think I have," replied Joe. "She's a beauty isn't she?"

"She sure is, you lucky git!" replied Pete without a hint of malice.

"Well, I would say let's go celebrate with a drink, but the pubs are shut now!" laughed Joe.

"Come and have a jar at my house then," smiled Pete, "I've got some cans in the fridge."

The pair of them reached Pete's car where it was parked and cheerfully drove off.

Sally could hardly keep her mind on her work the next day; she was so looking forward to seeing Joe that evening.

"Auntie Sally!" Davey gave her overall a tug. "Auntie Sally! Why do you keep smiling like that? Are you thinking of something nice?"

Sally looked down into the brown eyes she loved so much and smiled again.

"Yes Davey, something very nice! But I will tell you about it later. Right now we need to get you ready for school."

****

The date went very well. Sally and Joe got on like a house on fire. They went to a pub down the road and just talked and talked. Sally loved to look at him, he was just so cute! She loved his cheeky dimpled smile. It threw her a bit to find out he was only seventeen, two years younger than her, but she decided it didn't matter. She loved being with him.

Joe, for his part, was in love. It consumed him completely. When he was with her he couldn't take his eyes off her; he adored the sound of her voice, her tinkling laughter, the way her eyes lit up when she smiled. Even if her mouth didn't smile, her eyes did; he could always tell when she was smiling. And her figure was lovely too; she was slim but shapely. He dreamed of being able to touch her, of making love to her. When he wasn't with her, she filled his thoughts so much that he longed to be with her all the time. He would rush home from work, get changed, bolt his tea and fly out of the door to go and meet her, his mother Gladys laughing indulgently as the door slammed shut behind him. She had never seen her lad like this before! Mind you, she could understand it because when she met Joe's lass she was immediately taken with her. She could see that Sally was lovely and a very caring person. Sally treated her with respect and friendliness, showing interest when they talked and never showing that she was bored with the talk – and the way she loved those children she looked after! Her eyes positively glowed when she talked about them! But deep down, Gladys was worried; after all, Sally was two years older than her lad....

Of course, once Joe came on the scene, he became part of the family gatherings at Manvers, with Jim, Mo, Sally and Davey. He joined in the mad games and the picnics. There were many more times when Joe was there when Davey wasn't and he and Jim got on extremely well. They shared a love and knowledge of cars. Maureen and Sally would watch them both lovingly as 'the boys' sat and discussed engines and other things they knew nothing about.

Sometimes, if Sally and Joe went out on a Friday night on her weekends off, she would stay the night at Beaumont House, then she and Davey would walk down to Joe's house in the morning and together they would catch the bus that would take them up to Manvers to spend the day with Jim and Maureen. Sometimes they would all go to Dinmore Woods together, or up into the Black Mountains. Davey loved going out in Granddad Jim's car – and Sally and Joe loved to sit squashed together in the back seat with Davey! They had so much fun together and it seemed that things were going really well - until Joe had his 18th birthday.

Sally had bought him a gift; it was a silver cigarette lighter in the form of a pistol. She took it over to him at his home. He invited her to come to his party. She went to the party, which was being held at his home. It wasn't really so much a party, just a gathering of a few of his friends. Pete was there, and Sally greeted him with pleasure. There was music and a few people dancing. She was standing watching, when a young man came up to her. He was good looking, she supposed. He had dark blond hair which curled slightly at his collar, and blue eyes, with the longest lashes she had seen on a man! He was about five feet ten inches tall and was dressed in jeans and a hand-knitted Arran sweater.

"The name's Evan," he said to her, looking at her smoulderingly.

"That's nice for you," she replied lightly.

"Dance?"

"'Spose so."

Sally danced with him for the rest of the song. She scrutinised him from under her eyelashes. He was very erect and he was a good mover. There was something about him that she found fascinating somewhat against her will. She wanted to get away when the song finished but he stopped her.

"Can I get you a drink?"

"Er, yes. Ok. Thanks." She wanted him to go away. Where was Joe?

Evan came back with her drink alarmingly fast.

"Shall we sit down?" He led the way over to the settee. She sat down and he sat next to her. He asked her about herself so she told him a little and that she worked at Beaumont House. He put his arm along the back of the settee and she felt a tingle at the light contact with the back of her shoulders; she was getting jumpy. He attracted her but she also found him arrogant. She told him she was going out with Joe. He seemed to ignore that, which annoyed her. She looked around for Joe – where was he? Then she saw him watching her with Evan, glowering. Oh dear! She excused himself and went over to him, tucking her arm through his.

"I've been waiting for you to rescue me!" she hissed in his ear. "Get me away from that creep! Who is he? He thinks too much of himself!

"That's Evan. He's a mate of mine. Pete, Evan and I often go around together," Joe explained. "He's okay – he likes to get round the girls, but he's all right really."

"Well, I don't like him!" Sally was adamant. "Come and sit over here with me and keep him away from me." She led the way to the sofa and they sat down together. Joe was secretly very pleased that she didn't seem to like Evan; he was a 'ladies' man' and women of all ages seemed to fall under his charm. When the evening was over, Joe walked Sally back to Beaumont House and kissed her goodnight. She put her arms around his neck and nuzzled his face.

"Happy birthday Joe," she whispered. "And thank you for inviting me to your party."

"I will see you next Friday evening," he said and she nodded. "Goodnight Sal."

"Night Joe," Sally stood on the doorstep and watched him as he walked down the road and waved when he turned round to look at her before he disappeared out of sight.

Sally shut the door and sighed. She really liked Joe and had been happy with him, but now thoughts of Evan kept intruding into her mind…

****

Friday came, and Sally was happily getting ready to go out with Joe. She had largely been able to push thoughts of Evan from her mind and convinced herself that she was not likely to see him again. As she was changing in her bedroom, Andrea poked her head around the door.

"Sally! There's someone here to see you."

"Who is it?" Sally asked puzzled. Andrea would have said if it was Joe.

"Dunno. You'd better come down and see. He's in the hall."

"He?" Sally mused.

"Yes, it's a very attractive fella!" Andrea giggled. "You lucky girl!"

Sally was ready to go out with Joe, so she picked up her bag and her coat and went downstairs. No point in having to go back up after she'd seen who this was. To her surprise, it was Evan!

"What are you doing here?"

"I've come to take you out," was the reply.

"But I'm going out with Joe."

"Oh Joe is just a young lad, he's too young for you. You need a real man, you're coming out with me!"

"But he will be here very soon," Sally was agitated. She didn't like this guy; he was arrogant and so self-assured. She was annoyed that he took it for granted that she would go with him. But he did attract her, almost against her will. Being very unworldly, she had never come across anyone quite like him.

"Come on," Evan headed towards to the door and, hardly knowing what she was doing, Sally followed him. When they got outside, she said,

"Joe will be almost here now, we will meet him!"

"We will go down the back way; he will not come that way," was the reply. Sally still didn't really want to go with him but somehow she went. A few minutes later, to her horror, who should they see walking towards them, but Joe.

Sally thought she would never forget the look on Joe's face as he walked towards them.

"What's this?" he demanded when he was close enough.

"Sally's coming out with me," Evan was firm.

"Sally?" Joe turned to her. "Are you really?"

"She is," Evan said, as if there was to be no debate about it.

"It's for Sally to decide," said Joe. "Do you want to go with him Sally? If you go with him now, that's it between us. Which is it to be?"

So much went through Sally's mind in those few moments; Joe was lovely, but really he was too young for her. Evan was her age and he was rather compelling. Hardly knowing what she was doing she turned to go with Evan. She saw the devastated look in Joe's eyes as he turned to precede them down the hill. She wished already that she had not made the decision that she had made but Evan had taken her arm and was hurrying her down the hill.

Later, she just could never explain why she went with Evan. The memory of those few moments, which changed the direction of her life, was destined to remain with her for the rest of her days....

Chapter 7

Plans

"I really like your family," Evan said as they walked together down the lane from Sally's parents' house. It was Boxing Day and they had just had dinner at Manvers. Sally had been on duty at Beaumont house on Christmas Day and so now they were having another day of celebrations with family.

"I'm glad you do, because they are very special people," she said seriously.

"I can see that. I think all the children at Beaumont House are just great too," he replied. "And you are so good with them; they obviously love you very much."

"Well, I love them! The other Aunties and I are like their parents; we should love them, they need to be loved. Just because they are in care there is no reason why they shouldn't be loved, it's not their fault they are in care. In fact, it's even more important for them to know that we love them; it can't be easy to be taken away from your parents and live in a great big house with loads of other children and strangers looking after them - although of course, we don't remain strangers for long."

They walked along in silence for a while.

"I like your family too," said Sally.

"They really like you," he assured her

"Do they?"

"Oh yes, they think you are really nice and they like you better than any other girl I've been out with that they have met. Not that they have met most of them!"

"Yes. Right." Sally thought about some of the stories he had told her and really was not surprised that his family hadn't met these girls! The thought made her shudder.

"Are you cold?" he was surprised as her involuntary shake. He tightened his arm around her. "Come on, let's go back."

Sally turned around with him and thought that it was just as well he couldn't read her thoughts.....

The year continued on and, as it got near to her birthday, Evan said:

"I think we should get engaged on your birthday."

Sally was surprised. They were getting engaged? He hadn't asked her to marry him!

"But you haven't asked me to marry you!" she said.

"Of course you're going to marry me!" he was surprised. "You belong to me; I'm not letting anyone else have you! As soon as I saw you I knew I was going to marry you."

"That's more than I thought!" Sally kept her thoughts to herself. She recalled how she had felt on the day she had met him at Joe's party.......oh Joe.....! She thought about Joe, thought about the look on his face that day when she had decided to go with Evan.....

She shook her head; don't think about Joe! She wouldn't stand a chance with him now, she knew that. She doubted that he would forgive her. She hoped he had moved on. It looked like she had.......

And so it was that Sally and Evan got engaged on her birthday. She chose a simple ring with a single diamond in a small star setting. She had very slim fingers and she preferred small and dainty rings. They didn't have an engagement party because they were aware they needed all the money they could save to put a deposit on a house. They set the date for the 21st August for the wedding.

Summer came and the children were broke up from school. One evening, Evan said,

"I want to take you down to the Gower. It is very beautiful there, you would love it. I grew up in Swansea and I'd like you to see the places I knew."

"I'd like that. When shall we go?"

"How about Wednesday? Perhaps we could take some children with us for a trip out?"

"That's a great idea. I'll have a word with Emily Matron."

And so it was that Evan and Sally set off for Swansea with Davey, Juanita and Belinda. Belinda's sister Jody wanted to go too but Emily decided that this time Belinda would go without her sister. They had a lovely day; no one was sick on the journey! Evan was a good driver; he had borrowed his stepfather's car.

When they arrived at the tiny beach, hidden away from the other beaches on the Gower, Sally thought it romantic perfection. There was a small narrow lane running down to it and there was actually a house on the beach! Not lived in now, by the looks of it, but still in reasonable condition.

The children tumbled out of the car and ran down the lane from where they had parked. Sally and Evan followed, carrying the picnic and towels.

"Look at that house, Auntie Sally!" called Belinda, "I've never seen a house on a beach before."

"Nor have I, Belinda. Let's look, shall we?"

They walked all around the outside of the periphery fence. It was an attractive little cottage. Sally's imagination ran riot, thinking of smugglers and dashing contrabands. But really, it was just a sad, abandoned little cottage.

Sally wondered what it would be like to live in such a house so very near the sea; in fact, on the same level as the sea! She decided that perhaps it might be rather dodgy in the winter, although Evan said the water didn't come up that high.

The children soon tired of the cottage and were soon enjoying the warm and soft sands. They all had a wonderful time in the sea and building sand castles and eating the picnic that they had brought with them.

"I'm sorry, kids, it's time to go." Evan stood up and shook the towel he had been sitting on.

"Oh, do we have to? It's so lovely here." Belinda said. "And we haven't quite finished our sandcastle yet."

Sally looked at the three children, who looked back steadily with large eyes. She laughed.

"Just a few minutes more, to finish. But we mustn't leave it too long because we will get into trouble with Aunty Emily if we are late back."

Evan and Sally joined in with the castle building; Evan added artistic embellishments which made it look even more real. Half an hour later, all five stood back and admired their handiwork.

"Do you think it will stay here, Aunty?" shy little Juanita ventured. "It's quite near the house."

"Well, it might well stay a while. Let's hope it will. Now, we really must be on our way. Perhaps we can get some chips somewhere in Swansea."

Once in the car they were drawing near to Swansea.

"Oh look! There's a fair!" Sally exclaimed. "If the fair is open, perhaps we can have a ride or two?"

Evan parked the car on an empty car park by the fair. The children ran to the Waltzers and Sally and Evan followed. Sally enjoyed it at first but it went on for far too long and she wished it would stop! Then Davey and Belinda wanted to go on another ride, which Sally always thoughts of as 'Octopus' but it wasn't called that. As it flung them from side to side, round and round, Sally really began to feel quite bad! As she was flung near the operator, she tried to plead to stop but was flung away too quickly! Evan wasn't on this one and she tried to send him pleading looks. Eventually, he got the message and finally managed to persuade the operator to stop the machine! Sally got off feeling very ill......

However, they bought chips at a nearby chip shop and Sally started to feel better, as did the children. The journey home was, thankfully, uneventful and Sally made a mental note never to go on a ride in an empty fair ever again!

Summer drew on and life at Beaumont House continued as usual with the children playing outside or the aunties taking their families out to town or to the Quarry or just for a walk. One day, as Sally was sorting clothes in the children's bedroom, a child came up looking for her.

"Aunty Sally, you are wanted on the phone."

Sally hurried downstairs to the office. It was Evan.

"This is a quick call, love. Do you want a house in Holly Avenue? I've got a workmate who is putting his house up for sale and if we want it he won't put it in the estate agents' hands."

Flustered, Sally said 'yes' and agreed to go with him to see the house that evening. She was pleased because she liked the houses there and had friends living in the same street.

So that was it! Suddenly, they had a house – and she hadn't even seen it yet!

That evening, Evan collected her and together they went to see the house. This was a row of modern terraced houses; they were only about six years old. It was higher up the road than her friends' house, but it was the same; it was even the same way round! This house was clean and the sitting room and kitchen were decorated nicely; the bedrooms had all the same wallpaper but in different colours! Obviously it had been done to make it look presentable for selling. It was fine; Sally was happy to have this one. In fact, she was thrilled to get a house in the very place she wanted. They would be able to have the keys a week before the wedding.

The reception was booked; the bridesmaids' dresses were nearly finished. Sally had already made her dress. She was now putting the finishing touches to the two older bridesmaids' dresses. Evan's younger sister, who was eight, was to be the other bridesmaid and her mum was having the dress made for her. Everything was set. Except Sally was having growing reservations about marrying Evan - she wasn't sure that she loved him enough to want to be with him for the rest of her life. In fact, sometimes, she didn't like him much at all. She wondered how she had managed to get into this situation.

It perturbed Sally somewhat when her mother and father expressed that they were worried about her marrying Evan and asked her not to marry him. They couldn't explain why; they just felt it was not right.

However, Sally felt she couldn't back out now; everything was ready for the wedding and more importantly, the house was bought. She had to go through with it didn't she?

Chapter 8

Married Life

Sally gazed up the minister's nose in despair. She knew she had just made the most awful mistake of her life. The minute she said 'I do' she knew she had done the wrong thing. She understood in a split second that the feelings of apprehension she had been experiencing these past few weeks were trying to tell her something that she already knew deep down – that Evan was entirely wrong for her. However, she had just made a promise before God; she was bound, she couldn't back out now. If only she'd had the sense to do it before it got to this stage.

In the congregation was Aunty Lillian and Aunty Andrea, and with them were a few children from the home; Sally had made sure that Davey was there; he looked very smart in his school uniform. On the way back down the aisle holding the arm of her new husband, Sally gave Davey a special smile and mouthed a kiss at him. He felt so very proud of her; she looked so lovely, just like a princess! And Davey wasn't too sad because he knew she was still going to stay working at Beaumont House and he would see her again in a couple of weeks.

"Beautiful wedding, Sally," her aunt Evelyn said to her at the reception, held in The Priory out in the country. Sally smiled and nodded.

"Glad you are enjoying it, Aunt." She kissed Evelyn and moved on to the next person. She so wished she could feel the same! She ate little, instead she moved around, talking to all their guests. Her new mother-in-law was very happy and thoroughly enjoyed herself. Lots of others remarked on the atmosphere, which was very friendly.

Sally had to admit that her bridesmaids did look lovely in their peach-coloured dresses with matching flowers in their hair. And The Priory was a gorgeous place for a reception; the grounds lent itself to the photos, taken outside.

The honeymoon was indeed everything she had feared. The daytimes were just fine; they had a lovely time exploring the area where they were staying in South Wales or drinking in a beer garden. The weather was glorious.

Night times, however, were a different story. Evan was not a considerate lover and Sally felt abused. He seemed to have no idea how she felt about it; he was always cheerful during the day and seemed to love being with her. In fact, he seemed like two different people, one during the day and the complete opposite at night. Sally longed to go home.

But of course, being at home was no better. But at least she could do things at home to help keep her mind off the nights. If only he would be a bit tender towards her it might have made a difference. She realised she had led a sheltered life and had no real idea what being married would be like but she couldn't bring herself to believe it should be like this; if you truly loved someone, surely you should treat them with love and gentleness?

The one bright spot in her life was her job at Beaumont House. Emily matron had arranged her shifts to fit in with Evan's. She would catch a bus at the bottom of her road and then walk up from the bus station. She still had her family there to love and care for; it made her feel human again when Evan made her feel less than human. She wasn't able to take Davey home anymore; Evan would not allow it, So Davey never saw her house, but sometimes she did take him to see her parents at Manvers, or Jim would fetch him to spend some time with them, as they understood that Evan would not allow Sally to take Davey out.

"Oh Jim," her mother would say, "I am so sorry that Sally is so restricted. I do wish she hadn't married Evan, I begged her not to."

Jim put his arms around her.

"I know love, we both did. We did our best. Now we can only be there for her if she needs us. In the meantime we can keep an eye on young Davey."

Jim and Davey became even closer during this time. Davey was almost ten now and was growing fast. Neither of them realised that the time was coming when Davey would no longer be able to come and visit them.

A few months into the marriage, Evan decided that he didn't want his wife to work, so, much against her will, she had to hand in her notice at Beaumont House. She was so sad to leave all the children. Davey clung to her.

"Oh Aunty Sally," he was struggling manfully not to cry. "I will miss you, do you have to go?"

Sally sat on the bed next to him and pulled him onto her lap, she put her arms around him. She was still thin as ever and pale.

"Don't worry darling, I will still see you and you will still visit Granddad Jim and Granny Mo. Dry your tears now; be brave for me."

She was crying herself; it was breaking her heart to go. She pulled out a handkerchief and wiped his face, then her own. They stayed for a few minutes, holding onto each other as they sat on his bed. Emily happened to walk past at that moment; she thought afterwards she would always remember the picture of the young woman, the child on her lap almost as big as her, holding his dark head to her chest, rocking backwards and forwards a bit and the tears running down her cheeks. Emily's soft heart ached for this girl; she had an idea the marriage was not a happy one, although Sally never said anything. It was just that something vital was now missing in Sally, who had always seemed to sparkle with love, fun and humour; the spark was definitely gone. And now she had to leave the job she loved, leave these children who were her life. Emily went on her way; she knew the two needed these moments. She saw John heading towards his bedroom and called to him.

"John! Can you come here to me a moment? There's a little job I'd like you to do for me."

John headed towards Emily and walked with her down the corridor, away from his bedroom.

****

When Sally had left her work at Beaumont House, things got harder for her. Christmas came and went; then in the New Year Evan's factory where he worked was running into problems so he was put on short time. This meant he had more time at home. Sometimes they went to a dance on weekends and that was good, Sally enjoyed that, especially as he always drank too much and ended up completely unable to do anything once they got home.....

He had palled up with his best man again and they started going out together. Sally didn't mind that as it left her to have peaceful evenings to herself. The demands on her were getting less and she appreciated it. Until one night when she was enduring another onslaught and he called her Dawn....

"You just called me Dawn!" she said. "Who's Dawn?"

"Dawn? I never said that," he denied.

"Oh yes you did! I heard it plainly, "Who is Dawn?"

"Oh, just someone I was talking to tonight when I was out with Nick," he replied casually.

"I see," she thought she did see too....

He turned away from her then and settled down to sleep.

In the morning, she asked him again who Dawn was. Evan did not lie well. She could see straight away he was not telling the truth when he said he'd just met her last evening.

"So, how many times have you had sex with her?" She asked.

He was silent. She sighed and went into the other room.

Life went on as usual; then Sally started feeling ill...was she pregnant?

She was indeed pregnant and when she told Evan he was over the moon! He started treating her much better, was diligent and cared for her. Even his lovemaking became more gentle – mustn't hurt the baby! Sally thanked God, even though she was feeling so ill; she felt constantly sick all day.

Things improved; Evan was able to go back to work full-time and Sally started going to ante-natal clinics. She was very happy about the baby and even though she hated knitting, she started making things. Together, she and Evan picked out a cot and a pram for the baby and other smaller things they would need for it. It was a lovely time and the happiest they had been together so far. Sally pushed thoughts of Dawn away. She knew he wasn't seeing anyone now; he seemed to prefer being at home with her in the evenings.

It didn't last though, it couldn't, could it? Not with Evan. The time was coming when her tummy was so big that sex was difficult. He didn't bother her much, but he did start going out again....

Sally sighed to herself; she knew what he was up to. She wondered if it was Dawn, or someone different. She rather suspected it would be someone else – Even liked variety.

One night, she was still up when he came home.

"Don't look at me like that," he said.

"You're doing it again, aren't you?" she remarked.

"If a man can't get his pie at home, he will get it somewhere else," he replied and stomped off to bed, leaving Sally staring after him, stupefied.

****

Sally decided to ignore Evan's behaviour. She was getting very near her time and she was feeling even more poorly. Her doctor at ante-natal clinic was very concerned about her; her haemoglobin levels were very low. He kept giving her iron tablets but they made her stomach feel bad. She just wanted to get it over with.

Two weeks after her expected delivery date, Sally was wearily attending clinic. She saw a doctor she had never seen before. After examining her carefully, he announced that she was not due yet, the baby was too small. It would be another month! Sally came out in a daze. A woman she knew was serving teas from the WRVS cafe. Mrs Watkins noticed how dazed Sally looked and hastened out of her stall to help her into a chair.

"What's the matter, Sally dear?" she asked, very concerned.

"I can't believe it! The doctor says my baby is not due for another month yet – and I thought I'd passed my due date two weeks ago! He says the baby is too small to be born yet."

Mrs Watkins gave the girl a cup of tea.

"Get that down you dear, it will help you feel better," she soothed, "They think they know everything, but they don't. Your baby will be born when it's ready."

Sally sipped the tea gratefully. The warmth seeped through her and she felt stronger.

"Thank you so much. I needed that. I had better be getting home now. I will see you soon."

Not ten minutes later, Sally climbed aboard the bus and waited for it to leave. Not long after, the bus set off at the appointed time, four o'clock. The bus started up and Sally experienced a sharp pain that grabbed her straight in the stomach - oh no! It can't be! It was. Every time the bus stopped and started again she got a pain. She got off the bus at her stop and was immediately doubled over in pain. She walked up her road, bending forward every few minutes until the pain passed. She never expected anything like this; the pains were supposed to start gently round the back and gradually get stronger and move round to the front....

Fortunately, Evan was due home very soon; his shift ended at four. When he got home, he got her some tomato soup as that was the only thing she felt she could eat. Unfortunately, it wasn't long before it came back up.

Evan phoned the hospital; when he told them Sally had been having pains every few minutes from the start, they said she should come in. So she got her case and Evan drove her to the hospital. On examination, it was established that the baby wouldn't be born just yet, so they sent Evan home and gave Sally Pethadin and told her to try to sleep - fat chance with the pains coming every few minutes!

Sally knew the baby was going to be a breech birth, but no one had warned her what this was going to mean; that was the reason why the pains had been every few minutes from the start and why, later on, the 'bearing down' went on for so long. At one point, she felt something tickling her between her legs and went to put a hand towards it.

"Don't touch, my dear, it's the baby's foot," the midwife told her and Sally snatched her hand away as if it had been stung. A foot! Her baby's foot was already born. A giggle bubbled up inside her, but before it could come out, another pain hit her and she gasped instead.

When the time finally came, the actual birth was very easy; she didn't realise it as the midwife gave her an episiotomy to ease the head out. When a baby is born head first, the head pushes the uterus open; with a breech birth, that can't happen, so a cut has to be made to help the head come out. The baby girl was laid on Sally's stomach whilst the cord was cut and then she was wrapped up in a cover and given to Sally to hold. The baby was beautiful; because her head had not been squashed during birth, she was round and pink and lovely. Sally fell in love straight away with her baby and she knew her name had to be Jessica.

The midwife eventually took Jess away to weigh and bathe her. She covered Sally up and left her to rest. She had to await the doctor who had to stitch her up. Sally drank her tea, which was awful, being hospital tea, but it was lovely, just what she needed! Then she drifted off into sleep, dreaming that she had yet to give birth to her baby.....

The doctor eventually came, looking dishevelled and sleepy; Sally felt sorry for him, he had obviously been woken from sleep. She was embarrassed having a man sitting between her legs and made jokes about him having to come and do sewing in the middle of the night!

Soon she was in the ward and was thankful to sink into sleep. The morning came and she was feeling peculiar, so weak she could hardly move....

A nurse came and Sally barely heard what she was saying; she was floating away....she felt so light......

She became vaguely aware that things were happening around her; voices, far away, faces came into view then back out again....she was feeling so weak, so sleepy......

At one point, Evan was there; she was aware of his face for a moment, and then sank again into nothingness, although she thought she could hear something.....

Evan was frantic; Sally was dying! Unrealised, she had been bleeding the rest of the night after she'd been brought to the ward. Now, she was slipping in and out of consciousness; they had hooked her up to a blood drip. He had been horrified when he had come to the hospital in the morning as they had told him to. Sally was lying, pale and still in the bed, with blood being fed into her through a drip.

"Don't die Sal, please, please don't die." he pleaded as he sat at her bedside, holding her hand.

They brought the baby in to see him, and as he held the tiny girl in his arms he was absolutely head over heels in love; he'd never seen anything so perfect; he could hardly believe this was his flesh and blood. He had never loved Sally so much as he did now, for giving him this little person and he so needed her to live; to stay with him and their baby. He had always known she wasn't strong, but now he saw just how fragile she was and he also realised in part that he hadn't treated her very well......

The blood transfusions did their work; Sally gradually recovered and she actually had some colour in her cheeks as she now had some really good blood in her body. She and the baby had to stay in hospital for ten days. During that time she learned how to bath the baby and breast feed her. Having worked at the children's home she was already very efficient at folding and putting on nappies. She also had to have her stitches taken out when it was time, which was not very pleasant.

At last it was time to go home and Evan came to fetch them; he carried the baby proudly in her carry-cot into the car and handed Sally tenderly into the passenger seat. She was exhausted by the time they got home but was glad to be out of the hospital.

The first year of Jessica's life was the best year of Sally's and Evan's marriage. He was so proud of his beautiful baby girl and for her part she adored her daddy. When he was at home, Sally didn't get a look in! But she didn't mind; she really enjoyed seeing the two of them together. Evan was also much tenderer with her, treating her more gently, was more considerate both in day to day living and in bed. He loved to take them out and show them off. Evan's parents and his little sister also loved Jess and really enjoyed being visited by them. Life was happy at last.

Chapter 9

A Miracle for Marjorie

While Sally was going through her marital problems, Marjorie had a secret. It was something she wanted to shout from the rooftops but she knew she had to keep quiet about it, or someone would put a stop to it if they could.

In fact, Marjorie was planning to get married. She had met someone quite wonderful – trouble was, her Mr Wonderful was a parent of two children at Beaumont House – Davey and John, no less. She had met him on one of the rare occasions he came to see his sons – and my, was he good looking! Marjorie took one look at him and decided that this was Something That Had to Be. So she set to on her plans.

She started to take John home with her on her days off; she said it was to compensate him for Sally taking Davey to her home. Marjorie's parents were just as taken with John as Sally's were with Davey. They spoiled him, buying him things, taking him out to places. John loved all the things they gave him. Pity he had to leave them there when he went back to Beaumont House, how he would love to show them off to the other children, especially to Davey! John's nose had been put seriously out of joint when Aunty Sally started taking Davey home with her. It's true that sometimes she took him as well, as she thought it wasn't fair that he never went with them. Of course, he knew she sometimes took other children with her, but he knew she took Davey more often. If he was honest to himself, he really preferred to go to Aunty

Sally's with Davey; they had lots more fun there. But at Aunty Marjorie's he was the centre of attention – and John craved attention.

When Aunty Marjorie had first said she was going to take him out, he didn't really want to go, especially without Davey, but he soon got used to going and knew he could get her parents to give him anything he wanted, within reason. They even bought him a bike, which was his pride and joy. He soon was able to ride it, he had a good sense of balance. He would ride it up and down the pavement outside their house. It was a very quiet road so he was quite safe. He was careful never to go on the road anyway.

With the first part of her plan operating, Marjorie stealthily put into action the second part of the plan. She found out where the family home was, by sneaking into the office one day when Emily and Arthur were out. It was actually not all that far from her own home – how very convenient she thought. She took to walking past his house on her days off when she didn't have John there. She did this quite a while and then one day she had a stroke of luck when she happened to see the next door neighbour and struck up a conversation with her.

She casually mentioned that she was looking for a house in the area. The next door house never seemed to have anyone there – was it empty?

Barbara was only too happy to have a natter.

"Oh no dear, it's not empty, although it looks like it. It's owned by a man called Tony Adams and he's away a lot working."

"Oh right," said Marjorie, "What a pity! I always like the look of these houses and have always wondered what they are like inside," she continued innocently.

"Come and have a look at mine!" invited Barbara, "In fact, if you have time, perhaps you'd like a cup of tea? I was just about to have one."

"Thank you, I've love one!" Marjorie followed Barbara into her house. She dutifully admired the kitchen and the sitting-room, remarking on how spacious it was. And the dining room was a good size too, plenty of room for a family.

Barbara handed her a cup of tea and they sat down at the kitchen table together.

"I always sit in the kitchen, I don't know why really," she remarked. "It always seems more homely when I'm here on my own."

Marjorie agreed that it was indeed cosy and the kitchen had a lovely 'cottage' feel to it.

"Yes it does, doesn't it? Of course, Tony's kitchen isn't nearly as nice as this; he doesn't bother much with his house since his wife left."

"His wife left?" enquired Marjorie innocently. "Why? When? Did they have any children? I suppose she took them with her if they did."

"Oh no!" exclaimed Barbara, "She left the children too! It happened nearly three years ago now. She just upped and left, without any warning. Two sweet little boys they had – they were about five and six at the time. They came home from school; they had been picked up by her friend, to find the house empty. She had gone and left two notes, one for the boys and one for their father."

"How dreadful!" Marjorie acted appalled. "What happened to the children?"

"Well, I did my best to look after them before and after school until Tony came home from his work, but it got too much for me. And then there was the problem of what to do when he had to go away to work as he often had to do. They eventually went into care."

"Poor little boys; and their poor father as well," Marjorie was all sympathy. "And how sad for you too, I expect you were fond of them?"

"Oh yes! They were lovely boys! The older one, Davey, was such a good boy and tried so hard to look after his brother."

"And their father - how did he cope?"

"Oh well, it's difficult to tell with men isn't it? He is away a great deal now. He puts everything into his work. I suppose he doesn't see much point in being at home really. He has no one to come back to."

"Poor man - it must have been so hard on him to lose his complete family like that," Marjorie sighed, sipping her tea and politely refusing a proffered biscuit.

"Of course, his work was half the trouble," confided Barbara, "He was away so much, leaving her to look after the boys by herself. She was young; she wanted fun and attention." Barbara leaned forward conspiratorially. "She often had men there when he was away. I used to see them go in there of an evening and come out in the morning..."

"I bet you did," thought Marjorie. Out loud she said, "How perfectly dreadful!"

"Of course, I never said anything. Well, you can't can you?"

"No, that would be very difficult."

"I couldn't know that she would end up leaving him!"

Barbara was getting a bit upset now.

"I often wonder if I should have said something – whether it would have made any difference..."

Marjorie leaned forward and touched the older woman's hand.

"You couldn't have done anything. Saying something would have made things happen sooner than it did. Don't blame yourself. When someone is set on a course like that, there is little anyone can do to stop it."

Barbara looked at her gratefully.

"You really think so?"

"Yes, I do," replied Marjorie firmly. She got up from her chair.

"I'm afraid I have to go now," she said. "Thank you so much for the tea and the chat. Perhaps I can come and see you another time?"

"Oh yes my dear, I'd like that! You will be welcome any time."

Barbara walked down her path with Marjorie and closed the gate behind the young woman after she had gone through.

"It's been so nice talking with you Marjorie," she said. "Do come again soon."

"I will. Thank you. Bye for now!" Marjorie walked away, giving Barbara a cheerful wave as she went. She was very satisfied with a morning well spent. Having Barbara for a friend was just what she needed to attain her ultimate goal. Now, all she had to do was to somehow engineer a meeting with Tony Adams.....

****

As it happened, a few weeks later, Fate played into Marjorie's hands. She was on a long weekend off. On the Saturday her old school friend called her and asked if she fancied going out for a drink in the Broad Leys that evening. She was home visiting her mum and would like to see Marjie while she was here. Marjorie was pleased to say yes, so later the two young women went off to the Broad Leys, which wasn't too far away from where they lived. They sat at a table chatting and sipping their vodka and limes, when in walked a familiar figure. It was Tony Adams! Marjorie could hardly believe her luck! She watched him as he ordered a drink at the bar and then he glanced around for somewhere to sit. He headed towards their table as there were two empty chairs opposite the girls; the pub was quite busy that night.

"Is this seat taken?" he asked. Marjorie and Pat shook their heads. Tony sat down and took a long swig from his pint. He looked carefully at Marjorie.

"Don't I know you?" he said, puzzled.

Marjorie decided to play it cool.

"I'm not sure," she said carefully, looking at him studiously. My! He sure was good looking!

"Yes – I know! You work at Beaumont House!" he suddenly exclaimed. "I saw you when I went to see my sons – Davey and John."

"Why yes! Fancy you remembering me! I think we only met the once," Marjorie said coyly.

"I remember thinking how attractive you were," Tony remarked and he looked into her eyes. Marjorie looked back. Pat began to feel as if she shouldn't be there!

"I haven't seen you in here before," he mused.

"No, I don't come here much. I'm only here tonight because my friend here wanted to go out for a drink – I'm sorry, this is my friend Pat," Marjorie waved her hand towards Pat in introduction. "We have been friends for ever! We lived next door to each other and went to all the same schools together. Pat, this is Mr Adams."

"Tony, please call me Tony! How do you do Pat?" he nodded towards her.

"So....Tony.....do you come in here often then? Is this your local?" asked Marjorie, knowing full well he only lived up the road.

"Well, I work away a lot you know," he replied conversationally, "but I often pop in for a jar when I'm home. No fun in being at home on my own you know."

"No, I can imagine." Marjorie was sympathetic. "Of course, I'm at Beaumont House most of the time. It just happens to be my days off now."

"Yes, glad you were at home just when I was here," put in Pat, feeling she needed to join in the conversation – remind them she was there!

"So, you don't live here now then Pat?" Tony felt he should be polite and include her.

"No, I live and work in South Wales, Cardiff actually. I am a nurse there." Pat replied.

"So what was wrong with nursing here?" Tony asked.

"Nothing. I did work here for a long time, then I met a boy from Cardiff and we got married, so I went to live down there!" she laughed.

"Ah,you're married," he glanced at her left hand as if for confirmation.

"Yes. My mum hasn't been well, so I popped up for a couple of days to see her. Danny couldn't come with me this time; pressure of work you know."

"Yes, Pat's husband is a doctor," put in Marjorie, wanting to bring the attention back to her. "What do you do, Tony?"

"I'm an engineer," he replied. "I work for a firm that does work all over the country and sometimes abroad. In fact, they are getting more and more work abroad."

They sat chatting for an hour or so, finding lots of things to talk about. Tony knew a lot of people and got greetings from many of the other customers, who eyed the two young women he was with.

Eventually, Pat looked at her watch and said that she really should go home, that her mum would worry if she was out much longer. It was just about closing time anyway.

They stood up to go. Tony helped Marjorie and Pat on with their jackets and he walked out with them.

"May I escort you ladies home?" he asked gallantly. They hooked arms with him, one on either side, giggling and off they went, laughing, down the road. They delivered Pat to her door, bade her goodnight and then went on to Marjorie's house.

They stopped at her door. She turned towards him.

"Thank you for a fun evening!" she smiled her most beguiling smile on him. He looked into her eyes for a moment, and then he put a finger under her chin and tilted her head upwards and kissed her lightly on the lips.

"May I see you again Marjorie?" he asked he softly.

"Um, yes if you like," she acted cool but inside she was skipping around....

Are you still on your days off tomorrow?" he asked.

"I am actually."

"I don't suppose you would like to come and spend some time with me tomorrow? We could take a trip into the Black Mountains or something, take a picnic."

"That would be really lovely! Thank you, I'd like that very much."

"I will call for you – what time? About eleven?"

"Yes, that would be fine. I'll pack a picnic for us."

"Wonderful! Until tomorrow then......" He raised her hand to his lips and kissed it. Then he walked down the path towards the gate. Marjorie waved her hand at him, then turned and opened her door. She watched him walk away, and then closed the door.

"Yes!" she clapped her hands a couple of times in triumph. The scene was set!

****

The day trip to the mountains went very well. The day dawned bright and clear; it was going to be a perfect day to be in the mountains. Tony arrived dead on eleven o'clock. Marjorie was all ready, dressed in jeans and a shirt, with a sweater tied loosely by the sleeves around her shoulders. She had a cool box filled with all kinds of lovely things to keep them going for the day. Although in her late twenties, she still had a girlish figure, and Tony looked at her appreciatively.

For his part, Marjorie thought he looked gorgeous; he was also dressed in jeans and a casual shirt. The light colour of the pale blue and white shirt accentuated his dark colouring, so like Davey's.

He drove expertly with the confidence of one who does a great deal of driving. Marjorie stole a glance or two at his side profile as they went along. He had the window open a bit and the wind ruffled his hair. He was just so good looking! He felt her looking at him and turned to grin at her; he had the most disarming grin! Marjorie wondered how on earth his wife could leave him.....

"Penny for them!" his voice startled her.

"Oh, nothing much really," she replied, "I was just thinking how lovely it is to be able to come out on a day trip on such a beautiful day! I'm not usually this lucky on my weekends off!"

"We will have to do something about that then, won't we?"

Marjorie's heart leaped; was this really happening to her?

They enjoyed the day so much. They walked, or they sat and admired the incredible scenery and watched the mountain sheep wandering around. They smiled at other people also walking; families were there enjoying the great outdoors, there were couples like them, obviously discovering life together, there were elderly couples who had driven up there to partake of the scenery and watch life going by. It didn't seem to matter how many people were up there, it still seemed peaceful. Tony knew the area well and they found a place lower down where there was a crook in the road and a brook. Marjorie sat on a stone dangling her feet in the cool water, Tony beside her, also dangling his feet.

They had talked so much throughout the day about all sorts of things; getting to know each other. Just holding his hand was a delight; when he kissed her as they lay on a grassy patch just after having their picnic, Marjorie knew she was in love.

The sun was falling and it was becoming cool; they decided that it was time to go home. Marjorie was sad that the day was almost done. She sat in the car, watching as the mountainous scenery became just ordinary countryside, albeit beautiful Herefordshire countryside, which eventually changed into the outskirts of the city. All too soon, they were parked outside her house. Tony helped her out of the car and then got the now empty picnic hamper out of the boot. Handing it to her, he said:

"It's been a wonderful day Marjie."

"It certainly has Tony; thank you so much."

"I will be around for a while now; can I see you again please?"

"Yes of course! I am at home tomorrow, and then I'm back to Beaumont House on Tuesday."

"Perhaps I can see you tomorrow evening?" Marjorie almost laughed when she saw the hopeful expression on his face; he was as eager as her! It was like magic; she thought this would never happen to her.....

"Oh yes! I'd like that."

He took her in his arms then and kissed her. She returned the kiss with warmth. They parted reluctantly.

"Until tomorrow evening then; I will call for you about seven, is that ok?"

"I'll be ready!"

As she shut the door and leaned on it, she sighed. There was no doubt about it – she was in love!

Chapter 10

The Fruition

The next few months were, for Marjorie, like a merry-go-round of ups and downs. When Tony was at home and she could see him, she was up. When he had to work away, she was down. But she tried not to show it because she knew that he cared about her and didn't really want to be away from her. When he was away, she continued to take John home with her sometimes; when Tony was home, she didn't always, depending on what Tony was doing. She didn't want John to have any idea she was seeing his father in case he accidentally said something at the Home. Her parents had been sworn to secrecy. For their part, they were delighted – they might get John for a proper grandson!

Although Marjorie wasn't doing anything strictly wrong in seeing a parent of children in her care, she didn't want anything to stop it. When he was home and she was at Beaumont House, she always met him well away from the place so that no one ever saw them together.

Some of the other girls realised that she was seeing someone, but try as they might, they could not find out who it was.

For his part, Tony was in love too. He never thought he would find someone else after Sue left. Oh, he'd had many women; he was, after all, a very attractive man and had never been short of offers. He liked women, and they liked him and he was a great lover. But usually, once the chase was over and he'd had his way with them, he very quickly lost interest. Marjorie was an attractive woman, yes, but she was not beautiful as some of the women he'd had. But she had – well, she had something that seemed to hold him somehow. He never seemed to get tired of her; in fact, the more he had of her, the more he wanted. He felt he just had to have her for his own; for the first time since Sue he wanted to take the risk - and he knew that Marjie already loved his boys.......

They were having a meal at the Green Dragon; it was a very high-class restaurant in the city. They were celebrating a year since they met. Tony appeared a bit on edge, and Marjorie was starting to get worried; was he going to finish with her?

As they sat sipping their coffee at the end of the meal; Tony cleared his throat and she looked at him.

"What's the matter Tony? You've been acting strange all evening," Marjorie said, a bit sharply. "If there is something wrong, you need to tell me."

"Um, well, er," he began. Marjorie frowned, this was not like him at all!

"Yes?" she softened her voice, "What's the matter; you can tell me."

"Marjorie, would you marry me?" it came out in a rush.

Marjorie's eyes opened wider; was she hearing right? Had it actually happened?

"Marjorie? Did you hear me? Marjorie, I love you, will you marry me?"

"Oh Tony, this is so sudden! Can I think about it?"

She saw the expression on his face change to uncertainty and fear. She relented.

"I'm sorry to tease you dear – of course I will marry you. I thought you would never ask me!"

His expression changed in a moment as delight came into his eyes.

Tony took a small box from his pocket.

"If you don't like it, we can get another one," he opened the lid and offered it to her. She gasped; the ring was beautiful; a sapphire surrounded by diamonds in a cluster, so dainty.

"Oh Tony, it's beautiful!" she couldn't believe her luck!

"Try it on; we can get it altered if it's the wrong size."

Marjorie slipped it on her finger; it was a perfect fit.

"Made for you!" he laughed.

"Oh thank you my love," she smiled at him and held out her hand to admire the ring there. "I am so lucky. I will do my best to be a good wife to you and mother to your boys."

"I know you will my dear, but I didn't ask you because I want a mother for the boys. I asked you because I love you and want you to be my wife. I never thought I would find anyone else after Sue, but you have changed all that."

They left the restaurant and went back to his house. They made themselves comfy on the sofa and talked about plans. Marjorie said she only wanted a quiet wedding and she didn't want anyone at Beaumont House to know until after the wedding. Tony wanted the boys to be at the wedding, but Marjorie said it would be best if they were not there because they would have to stay at Beaumont House whilst their dad and new mother were on honeymoon.

"They might get upset about that; they will think they can come home to us straight away," she said. "And really, we need to do some work on the house; you've let it get dingy, Tony. We will make the boys' bedrooms nice so that it's all fresh and clean for them to come home to. If we make it different for them, it won't hold too many unhappy memories."

"Actually, I have a better idea," he said. ""Why don't I sell this house and we will choose a new house together."

Marjorie was pleased with that idea; it would save having to be friends with Barbara! And she liked the thought of looking around houses with him and choosing one together. It would really be theirs then.

"Come round to my house in the morning and we will tell my parents," she said. "They will be so pleased."

They were pleased; Tony would make a very good son in law they felt; they could see that their Marjorie was so happy – and they would have two ready-made grandsons, how lovely!

"Let's get married soon," said Marjorie to Tony. "But I shall stay at work for a while until we can find a house. I am not going to let them know until it suits me."

Tony thought this a good idea and they planned to get married just before Christmas with a view to having the boys back by the spring if they could get organised by then.

****

Tony and Marjorie got married on the first Saturday in December. It was a beautiful day; sunny but chilly. Marjorie looked lovely in a white calf-length dress with a fur trim around her shoulders. The small church that Marjorie attended was decorated with Christmas roses and Poinsettias and she carried a bouquet of Christmas roses. Her little niece, Sandra, was her only bridesmaid, looking very sweet in a frilly pink dress, carrying a small basket with more Christmas roses.

The reception was held in the British Legion club house, as Marjorie's dad was a member of the British Legion. It was just the right size for the small gathering of family from both sides. It was a good occasion. Marjorie's parents were overjoyed to see their daughter so happy. Her two brothers came; one, her brother Bob, was happily married and was Sandra's father.

The other, Richard, known as Dickie, was something of a 'black sheep' of the family. He had been married but had long abandoned his wife for another woman, and had had many women since then. He never stayed with anyone for long. He had also had many jobs and had lived all over the country doing various things. It was nothing short of a miracle he had turned up for the wedding! Marjorie stiffened when she saw him and braced herself against the feelings that the sight of him brought her. He was the last person she wanted to see on such a wonderful day as this. But she supposed that it was to be expected as he was her brother; however, she had hoped he wouldn't turn up...

"Couldn't miss your wedding sis!" he remarked to her cheerfully, as he planted a smacker on her cheek. Marjorie grimaced; his nearness and his touch made her skin crawl - and it was obvious he had already been drinking. She hoped he wasn't going to be a bother during the reception... however, he behaved himself and everything went well until it was time for the happy couple to leave for their honeymoon. Everyone stood and waved a cheerful goodbye to the happy couple as they drove away in Tony's car.

Marjorie's heart was full; she couldn't wait to start her new life as Tony's wife.

Chapter 11

A Worrying Time

Emily was extremely troubled. Marjorie had just been to see her and had given in her notice. It seemed that she had got married whilst she was on holiday. No one at Beaumont House had any idea that was going to happen. Now she knew why; Marjorie had married Davey and John's father, Tony Adams!

Normally, she wouldn't worry too much about such a situation, knowing that most of 'her girls' would be fine if they had married a parent of children in the home. But Emily was all too well aware of the potential problem in this case. The enmity between Marjorie and Davey was a worry. There wouldn't be anyone there in the child's home to protect him if things got out of hand. It was true there had been no incidents lately, but now that she knew about the marriage, Emily understood why. Marjorie had been so happy and had restrained herself from doing anything to Davey in case he said anything to his father on the occasions of his visits. Now she understood why the visits had become so much more regular lately too! For three years Tony Adams had barely visited his sons but now he was visiting them just about every month, sometimes more. Of course they were thrilled about this; they loved and needed their father. They obviously had no idea about the marriage; they would have said something if they had known. Davey would certainly have been very worried....

"We can't have the boys home yet because we are in the middle of buying a new house and we need to have time to get it ready for them," Marjorie told Emily. "I will be leaving Beaumont House at the end of January in order to give me time to start getting things ready. All being well, the boys could come home to us round about March or April."

Emily sat and thought for a while, wondering how on earth she was going to break the news to Davey. She wouldn't tell him yet; no point in letting the child have too long to dwell on bad thoughts and fears.

Abruptly, she pushed her chair back, left her office and went in search of Albert, who was in their flat on the top floor. She would make them a cup of tea and sit and calm herself.

"Albert!" she pushed the door of the flat open. Albert was sitting reading a book by the window. He looked up as she came in, taking in her distraught expression. He got up.

"Whatever is the matter dear?" he asked as he walked towards her. "Come and sit down and tell me".

"Oh Albert! You will never guess what has happened!" she looked at him, her eyes wide with distress.

"Tell me," he said, sitting down and gently pulling her next to him. He took hold of her hand.

"I have just come out of the office from talking to Marjorie," she said, "she has given in her notice!"

He relaxed. "Is that all? I would have thought you would be glad really."

"Well, normally I would have been - except she has got married."

"Has she indeed? She kept that a bit quiet. Just who is the brave bloke then?"

"That's the problem – it's Tony Adams, Davey and John's father!"

There was a silence; Albert was stunned. Then he let out a low whistle....

"My word! No wonder she kept quiet about it - poor Davey!"

Albert immediately realised that this was a potential disaster for the boy. His heart went to his Emily; he knew how much she loved each of the children in her care. He put his arm around her. She felt so tiny against him; he always felt so protective of her.

"Do you want a cup of tea, love?" he asked her. She nodded. Albert got up to make them one in the tiny kitchenette. All their meals were cooked in the kitchen downstairs but they had a kettle and could make drinks and small snacks for themselves here in their flatlet.

"So, what will you do?" he asked as he came through with the cups.

"Well, I'm certainly not going to tell him yet. Marjorie said they wouldn't be able to have the boys until March or April so there is no sense in letting Davey worry all that time."

"No, but you will," he thought to himself.

Out loud, he said: "No, there's no point at all."

The two of them sat side by side, sipping their tea, lost in their thoughts.

"I think, when the time comes for them to go, I might have to have a word with the child care officer, so she can keep an eye on the situation," said Emily thoughtfully. "Someone needs to keep an eye on him; I won't be able to do it once they are gone."

As Emily sipped her tea, she thought back to the time when Davey first arrived at Beaumont House. She thought of how Marjorie had taken against him, for no apparent reason. Then her thoughts moved on to Sally and recalled what a difference she had made in the little boy's life. Sally's marriage had removed her a bit from him as her husband had not allowed so much contact, but she had remained in Davey's life. Jim and Maureen Golding had been good to him too and she knew he loved them like grandparents. This marriage of the boys' father was going to remove Davey from just about everyone who was important to him, except his own father. But would his father be enough? Would his father protect him? Would his father believe it of Marjorie? Emily doubted it. Tony Adams was away from home a great deal; how long would it be before the glitter and shine of being married would wane and Marjorie would start taking her frustrations out on the boy? Emily had no doubt it would happen....

"You know Albert," she began thoughtfully, "I think I need to tell Sally about this."

Albert frowned.

"I don't think you should, Em," he said, "You know she is expecting a baby. We don't want her to have such a worry while she is carrying."

"Hm, perhaps you're right my love," Emily considered. "Perhaps I will wait until the baby is born.

She is bound to bring baby to see us. I will tell her then. Perhaps the boys will be gone by then and she will have to know they have gone. Her parents will need to know too."

"That's very true Em. They are going to be upset about it; they are very fond of Davey and they will miss being able to have him over there."

"They certainly will Albert my dear."

****

Sally's baby was due in March. When the whole month had come and gone, Emily started wondering why she had not heard anything. She decided to call Sally's mother.

"Hello, is that Mrs Golding? This is Emily Brown from Beaumont House."

"Oh yes Mrs Brown, how nice to hear from you. How are you?" Maureen was surprised.

"I am very well, thank you. I was just wondering about Sally because I know her baby was expected this month. How is she?"

"She is well now, but after she had her baby she was very ill for a while. She came close to dying you know; she lost a great deal of blood and was unconscious for a while and on a transfusion. They had to give her quite a good deal of blood I understand. She had a lovely baby girl called Jessica, she is a really beautiful baby. But it has taken time for Sally to get well again, which is probably why you haven't heard from her."

"I'm so sorry to hear that Sally was so ill," sympathised Emily, "but congratulations on your lovely granddaughter, Mrs Golding."

"Well, thank you very much Mrs Brown, we all love little Jess very much. How is Davey? It's been a while since we saw him."

Emily took a deep breath and let it out slowly.....

"I have to tell you about Davey, Mrs Golding," she explained, " His father has got married again and he and his young brother John are about to return home to live with him again."

"Well, that's good news for him and his brother!" Mrs Golding exclaimed. "Are they happy about it?"

"That's what I needed to talk with you and Sally about," Emily hesitated, "In fact I'm rather worried about it. You see, the woman their father has married is Marjorie."

"Marjorie? You mean Aunty Marjorie from Beaumont House?" Maureen was incredulous. "But how? How did it happen?"

"Well, I don't really know. She did it without our knowledge. She told me after she had married Mr Adams, when she handed in her notice."

"But Davey can't go and live with her - after the way she has treated him! Can't you do anything to stop it?" Maureen was distraught.

"I'm afraid there is nothing I can do, Mrs Golding. Mr Adams has the right to have his sons back home with him."

"How can I tell Sally? I can't tell her - she will be frantic!"

"Oh dear, yes, I know. I have been worrying about it ever since Marjorie told me three months ago. I have been worrying about Sally, but more about Davey!"

"Yes, I can understand that. Poor little fellow, having Marjorie for a step-mother," reflected Maureen. "I bet his father doesn't know anything about how she has treated Davey."

"I'm sure he doesn't. He seems to adore Marjorie. I have to say she seemed to have softened a lot before she left Beaumont House; maybe being in love has changed her." Emily said, hopefully.

"It may have done," Maureen was doubtful. "But how long will it last, I wonder?"

"Frankly, that's what I'm worried about too." Emily admitted. "I fully intend to warn the child-care officer about it when the boys go. Anyway, I felt that you and Sally needed to know."

"Yes. Thank you for telling me. I will tell Sally. Leave it with me."

Maureen put the phone down thoughtfully. She needed to talk with Jim about this.

When Jim came in for his lunch later than morning, Maureen told him about the phone call and the news. He was very concerned.

"Poor Davey, how terrible for him; I do hope he will be all right," he mused. "Mo, I don't think we should tell Sally about this; not yet. I think it will be too much for her. We can tell her he is going home to his father but we won't tell her who his step-mother is."

"Maybe you're right Jim."

"We will tell her next time she and Jess come to visit."

When he left her to go back to his workshop, Maureen sat for a while at the table and thought about Davey and how he had developed over the years they had known him. He was such a lovely lad, full of fun but very good. And he did so adore her Jim; he enjoyed being with her husband in his workshop and his shed very much. And he loved Sally, young as she was, she had been like a mother to him. Now he was going to live with that termagant Marjorie. How bizarre life was, to be sure, with all its unexpected twists and turns. She fervently hoped that things would turn out better for Davey than they all feared.

Chapter 12

A Shock for Davey

Davey was waiting impatiently for his father to arrive. John was waiting too. They had been told that he would be there at ten o'clock and it had already gone that by ten minutes. However, Davey knew that their dad was almost always late. He stood at the dining room window, watching for his father's car to come up the drive. A few minutes later, he saw it.

"He's here John - dad's here!" Davey ran from the room and careered towards the main hall. He was just in time to see Aunty Emily open the front door and his dad walk in. The door was shut behind him, and the two boys rushed to greet him.

"Dad!"

"Daddy!"

Tony opened his arms to hug both his boys. Then he held them away from him a little so he could look at them.

"I have some news for you boys," he said, looking from one to the other.

"You do, dad?" asked Davey. He could see that his father was very happy and smiling and his heart lifted. It was not going to be bad news then, although he could not imagine what it could be.

"Yes, my sons. You are going to be coming home to live with me again very soon! What do you think of that?" He asked them. He was pleased to see that their faces both broke out into wide smiles.

"We are? How come, dad?" Davey was puzzled.

"Well, I have got married again, so you have a new mother," Tony explained. "And we have bought a new house and have been getting it ready in order to have you come home to live with us."

Davey and John looked at each other, excited and pleased. This was indeed very good news!

Emily was watching the proceedings very carefully. Was Tony going to tell the boys who their new mother was?

Tony straightened up.

"Right boys, do you have your coats? I am going to take you to see our new house!"

The boys ran back to the cloakroom to fetch their coats and then ran back to their father. He held the front door open for them, and they followed him to the car.

"Your new mother is waiting to greet you at the house," their father told them. They climbed quickly into the back seat of the car and shut the door. They were very excited. They had both longed to go home to their father for simply ages and it was happening at last. Davey sat and thought about the time they had been brought to Beaumont House. John was too little to remember it, but he could, although it had been almost 5 years ago now. He wondered what his new step mother would be like and hoped she would be nice. Surely if his dad liked her, she would be?

It was quite a short ride to the new house, only about twenty minutes or so and the car soon pulled up outside a very pleasant – looking semi-detached house with a very pretty front garden. They got out of the car and as they walked up the path, the front door of the house opened and – no, no! What was *she* doing here? The woman of his nightmares was standing in the doorway, smiling. As if in a dream, Davey saw his young brother John run up to her and greet her.

"Aunty Marjorie! What are you doing here?" John said happily. "Have you come to help our new mother?"

"I *am* your new mother John!" Marjorie smiled and hugged him, looking over his head at Davey. She held her hand out towards him. "Davey – welcome!"

Davey hadn't realised it, but he had stopped short at the sight of her. He was only vaguely aware of his father gently propelling him towards the door. He stopped by the doorstep, too stupefied to go further.

"Look at him Tony – he is so surprised he can't move," laughed Marjorie. "Come away in boys! Come and look at our house and you will see your bedrooms. We have tried to make them look really nice for you."

It was indeed a lovely house and their bedrooms, of which they had one each, had been done out beautifully for them, with colourful bedspreads and pictures on the walls. Davey had to admit he really liked his room. John was so excited about everything that Davey's quietness went practically unnoticed. They all went out together to a nearby park after they had seen the house and they had a great time playing together on the swings and other things. Marjorie had prepared a picnic for them and they sat together under the shade of a large tree and ate the lovely sandwiches and cakes she had brought. In spite of the way he felt about her, Davey had to admit that Aunty Marjorie did seem nicer now; perhaps things were going to be all right...

When it started to get a bit chilly, they went home and the boys watched television while Marjorie prepared some dinner and they eventually sat down in the very pretty dining room and had a lovely meal of gammon, egg and chips, which the boys loved, followed by jelly and ice cream.

When they had eaten it was time to go back to Beaumont House. This time, Marjorie went with them, sitting in the front seat of the car next to her husband and the boys once again sat in the back. John chattered away happily during the journey, making them laugh.

Emily was there to welcome them back. She looked at Davey anxiously. He looked steadily back at her, his eyes unfathomable. Without a word, he walked past her and into the house. Emily eyed his back as he walked away from her; his back was slightly humped, his jacket was slipping off his shoulders and he was unheeding of it slowly sliding down further, his feet slapped the tiles as he hastened away towards the stairs......

She smiled at John and his father.

"So – have you had a good day out today John?" she asked him.

"Oh yes! We had a really great time! And guess what, Aunty Emily?" John was babbling excitedly. "You will never guess!"

"What's that John?" Emily looked at Tony over John's head enquiringly.

"Aunty Marjorie is our new mother! And we are going back home to live with her and daddy!"

"Well, I'm very glad that you are so happy John," Emily hugged him. "And have you seen your new house?"

"Yes! Me 'n' Davey are going to have our own rooms! It's great!"

"That all sounds lovely. Run along now and get your coat off. I expect Auntie Jean will be looking for you. It's nearly bedtime."

"Ok Auntie Emily. 'Bye daddy!" John kissed his dad then ran off in the same direction that Davey had gone.

Tony and Emily looked after him.

"So, it went well did it?" Emily asked him.

"I thought it went very well. We have had a lovely day together. However, I am rather worried about Davey's attitude – he doesn't seem altogether happy you know. He joined in with the fun but sometimes I caught him unawares and he had an expression on his face which I couldn't work out. I don't think he is that pleased to be coming home."

"Well, you have to remember that he bore a lot on his very young shoulders when his mother left. He is older than John and remembers more. Perhaps he is afraid it might all go wrong again," Emily was being diplomatic. How could she tell Tony that it was because Davey hated the woman who had become his stepmother? And that she hated him?

"Yes, you are perhaps right. Davey has always been a sensitive child. I will have to keep an eye on him. I'm sure he will soon see that things will be well. Marjorie will be a wonderful mother for them. John obviously loves her; well of course, she is already like a mother to them, being their housemother for the past four years."

"Yes. Well, I must get on with my work now, if you will excuse me, Mr. Adams?"

"Of course. And I mustn't leave Marj sitting in the car any longer." He made to leave and she followed him and opened the door.

"Oh, by the way," she said, "How long will it be until you have the boys?"

"Very soon now I hope," he replied. "I am seeing the Child Care Officer tomorrow to see how the procedure is progressing to have them back."

"Very good, I have no doubt I will soon hear from her then. Goodbye for now, Mr Adams."

Emily shut the door behind him and sighed. Then she headed towards the kitchen, she so needed a cup of tea.

****

For the next few days, Emily observed Davey. He was very quiet and when the other children played he just sat in the room, not joining in. He went to school, did everything he should but without enthusiasm. His housemother, Auntie Jean, came to her one day and expressed concern that he was being so quiet and eating very little. Emily explained the situation to her very briefly.

"Oh my goodness - poor Davey!" Jean was horrified. She was new, having replaced Marjorie so she did not know her predecessor, but she had heard quite a few stories. Jean had a kind heart and took great care of her 'family'. "Is there nothing we can do about it, Auntie Em?"

"I'm afraid not, Jean. The only thing I can do is ask Miss Mason to keep an eye on things, which she will have to do for a while anyway once the boys have gone home. And pray."

"Well, from what I have gathered, Davey has suffered enough already. What about Sally? Does she know about this?

"Well, I have spoken to Sally's mother because Sally is not on the phone. And she has been very poorly following the birth of her baby. Mrs Golding is very worried about Davey as we are."

"I'm sorry to hear that Sally has been ill. I wondered why we have not seen her lately. Davey has been asking for her you know."

"No, I didn't know! We must see what we can do to let him see her. I will get onto it."

"Right. That would be good; it might help him to see her. I'd better get back to my work. Thank you, Auntie Em."

"Thank you, Jean. See you later."

Thoughtfully, Emily reached for the phone.

"Hello? Could you put me through to Miss Mason please?"

****

Catherine Mason knocked on the door of Beaumont House. It was opened by Albert Brown, who welcomed her and ushered into the office. Emily Brown was there and stood up to greet her. They shook hands and Catherine sat down in the proffered seat.

"I have here the completed paperwork to get Davey and John Adams back to their home, Mr and Mrs Brown. Their father and I will come and fetch them on Monday morning. I think you will find that everything is in order now for their release back to their father."

Emily took the paperwork and laid it on her desk.

"Thank you, I will look it over later. I'm sure it's all fine. There is, however, a matter which is rather delicate that I wish to discuss with you."

"That sounds very serious!" Catherine looked sharply at Emily, then at Albert. He was looking serious too. What on earth could this be about?

"Yes. It certainly has the potential to be serious. Which is why I asked you to come and see us, Miss Mason," Emily pressed the finger-tips of her two hands together, resting her elbows on the desk in front of her.

This had the effect of moving her nearer to the woman sitting on the opposite side.

"This is going to be rather tricky to explain to you, but I will have to just come out with it. You are aware of who the boys' new stepmother is?"

"Why yes of course! She used to be a housemother here, didn't she? Is there a problem with that?" Catherine's eyes were questioning.

"Well, the fact is, Marjorie, now Mrs. Adams, was in fact Davey and John's housemother. Quite how she managed to meet and marry Tony Adams I'm not really sure. If I had been aware of the relationship I would have tried to stop it."

"Why? No law against a member of staff marrying a parent is there?" Miss Mason was puzzled.

"No, of course not. It's just that in this case, it would have been better not. You see, Marjorie and Davey do not get along at all well. In fact, more than that, they thoroughly dislike each other and Davey so often got into trouble with her – and, I'm afraid, she often was, shall we say, less than kind to him. I had to intervene on a few occasions when she was punishing him for something."

"Well, if a child does wrong, he should be punished, shouldn't he?" Miss Mason observed.

"Of course. It's just that he often got blamed for things that actually he didn't do and Marjorie would never listen to reason. And she was rather free with her hands."

"Oh....I see," Catherine was thoughtful.

"What I am saying to you, Miss Mason, is that I am strongly suggesting you need to keep a close eye on things once the boys have gone home. I've no doubt it will be all right at first, she will want to make a good impression on her husband. But, I think I'm fairly accurate when I say that leopards rarely change their spots...."

"Hmmm," Catherine's eyes narrowed. "Well, thank you for sharing your concern with me, Mrs. Brown. "I will see what I can do to keep an eye on the situation. Let's hope that being married and so on will have a good effect on Marjorie and she will turn out to be a good mother."

"I sincerely hope so, believe me. For Davey's sake, I hope so."

Catherine Mason stood up to leave.

"Right. Well, I will see you at eleven on Monday then, when we come for the boys. Goodbye Mrs. Brown."

"Goodbye, Miss Mason."

Albert saw her to the door. Catherine got into her car and carefully reversed in order to drive out.

"Oh blow it!" she thought, "And I thought this was going to be a straightforward getting the children home business. It's not going to be straightforward at all! This is going to mean more work for you, Cath my girl!"

Albert shut the door and went back into the office. He and Emily looked at each other.

"Albert, somehow I get the feeling that Catherine Mason is going to let us down," observed Emily sadly.

"I fear you may just be right, my dear," was his answer.

Chapter 13

Painful Partings

A week after the first phone call from Emily Brown, Maureen had another one. She waited for Jim to come home from work. She let him have his wash and change his clothes; he always came home so dirty even though he wore overalls!

When they were sat at the table together eating, Maureen said:

"Jim, I've had another call from Mrs. Brown at Beaumont House. Davey and his brother are going home on Monday."

Jim looked up. "Oh yes? That was sooner than I thought it would be"

"Yes. The thing is, Davey has been very upset and withdrawn since he found out about who his stepmother is. And he has been asking for Sally."

"We will go and see her when we've had tea, Monsie," said Jim. "We need to talk with her. She will want to see him."

"Yes dear, you are right."

They finished their meal in silence, each lost in their own thoughts, but thinking of the same things....

Sally was surprised to see her mum and dad; they didn't usually call round in the evenings. They came in and her dad immediately went to take baby Jess off Sally for a cuddle, crooning away to her. Jess treated him to her best windy smile and waved her arms about. Jim was besotted with her. Maureen smiled at him indulgently.

"Sally, we have I'm afraid, come to give you some news that you will be upset about," she began.

Sally looked serious. "What's up?"

"We have had a phone call from Mrs Brown at Beaumont House. "It's about Davey."

"Davey? What about him - is he all right?" Sally's eyes were wide with panic.

"Well, he is well, but he's not all right," replied her mother.

"What's happened?"

"He and John are going to live back home with their father. They are going on Monday."

"Well, that's not so bad, although we probably won't get to see him again, which is sad," Sally's eyes wandered to the small shelves on the wall. Amongst the small ornaments on them was her tiger.

"There is more I'm afraid. His dad has got married again – and he has married Marjorie!" Maureen looked at her daughter, waiting for her to realise the significance, which she did, immediately.

"Oh! Oh, tell me you are joking!" Sally looked from her mother to her father. Both were looking at her very seriously. "You're not joking are you? Oh no - poor, poor Davey."

She sank down on the settee, tears running down her cheeks.

Her mother sat down beside her and took her hand.

"Sally! Emily Brown says that he is really upset and withdrawn. But he's also been asking for you."

"I must go to him! Can you take me? When can I see him? If he is going on Monday there isn't much time." Sally stood up again, as if to go at that moment.

"Mrs. Brown has said we can have him tomorrow. As soon as dad has finished work we will come for you and we will go up there," Maureen looked at her daughter sympathetically. "I know you are worried about him love, but you have your own baby to think about and look after. You can't take on all the problems. It may be that it will be all right for Davey with Marjorie. Perhaps she will have changed. Perhaps being married will have softened her. You are going to have to help Davey to try to see it that way."

"I suppose you are right; I will try my best to help him be more positive," replied Sally. "But, as regards Marjorie, I hope she will have changed. But, somehow, I doubt it."

Sally didn't sleep at all well that night and when she did her dreams were very troubled. It was a long night at she tried to keep as still as possible so that she didn't wake Evan. At least she was glad that he was going with his mate to see Hereford United play the next afternoon which would leave her free to go to Davey. She was so glad when the morning came. At least she could get on with looking after Jess and doing other things which would keep her mind busy

****

The large blue door of Beaumont House was opened by Emily, who was all smiles to see baby Jess.

"Oh, isn't she sweet?" Emily peeked into the shawl wrapped round the baby.

"Would you like to cuddle her?" asked Sally and put the baby in Emily's arms.

"Hello little one," matron crooned to Jess. "Would you like to go find Davey, Sally? I think he's up in their room. We will look after the baby."

"Yes, I will go now," said Sally and headed off immediately towards the stairs. In no time she was at the door of Davey and John's bedroom. The door was slightly ajar and she pushed the door open further. Davey was sitting on the side of his bed. He had a book in his hands, but she could see he wasn't reading; he was just staring into space.

"Davey love," Sally's voice was gentle. He looked up, startled to see her. She saw tears well up in his eyes, which he struggled manfully against for a moment, and then he flung himself into her arms, sobbing.

"Aunty Sally! I-I thought I wouldn't see you again!" Sally held him, stroking his hair and murmuring to him; "There now, it's all right, my love, don't cry, I'm here now."

She sat, as she had many times before, holding him, rocking slightly, "There now, cry it all out now, don't worry, it's all right."

She held him until the sobs quietened, still stroking his hair and rocking. She closed her eyes as if to ward off the pain that assailed her; the pain her little boy was in, the pain that she couldn't do anything much to help him, to protect him... What would become of her boy?

When he had at last stopped crying she said; "there now, dry your eyes, we are going out. Granddad Jim and Granny Mo are here to take us back to Manvers – and there is someone you need to meet!"

Davey dried his eyes and then went to the bathroom to splash his face with some water. With the resilience of the young, he was now happy and looking forward to spending an afternoon with Granddad Jim, Aunty Sally and Granny Mo. Sally knew that she would be able to talk with him during the afternoon, or if not, when they brought him back.

They went downstairs, to find Jim and Mo and Aunty Emily surrounded by children and adults in the spacious hallway. Children were clamouring to see something and the housemothers were lifting smaller ones up. As they got closer, Sally said to Davey,

"And here is who I want you to meet." She took the baby from Emily and showed her to Davey. "This is my baby, Jess."

She watched as Davey solemnly looked at the baby and he took one of her hands. He held his finger out and smiled as she gripped it with all of her tiny fingers.

"She is very small isn't she, Aunty?" he looked at Sally with his big brown eyes and she nodded and smiled.

"She is, but she is already growing very fast."

"Right." said Jim, "Are you ready, Davey lad? Let's go."

He took Davey by the hand and led him towards the door. The two women followed them out, waving goodbye to the other children shouting their goodbyes to them.

They had a lovely afternoon together; the weather was beautiful for April and they decided to go for a walk in Queen's Wood and take a look at the bluebells and other spring flowers there. They had an ice cream which they bought from a van in the car park and enjoyed eating them as they walked around. Sally had the baby in her carry-cot pram which was easy to put in the car. Jess loved looking at the trees waving in the breeze above her and happily waved her arms about. Davey was fascinated by her and kept coming back to look at her. Then he would run off again to discover something else. He and Jim wandered off together, then after a while they re-joined the women. They reached the Lookout and duly admired the scenery and picked out the landmarks shown on the Lookout rock. Then they set off on the walk back and were thankful to eventually get back into the car.

Tea at Manvers was just as a Saturday tea should be with crispy rolls and a lovely cake. Davey as usual enjoyed it and had fun watching the wrestling on television with Granddad Jim while the tea was being prepared.

After tea, Sally took Davey for a while into the small sitting room because she wanted to talk with him. She decided to come straight to the point.

"Davey, I understand you are going home to live with your dad again – and that your stepmother is Aunty Marjorie."

She felt her heart drop to her toes when his head drooped and he nodded.

"I don't need to ask you how you feel about that," she continued. "I can see how you feel and I understand completely. But it may turn out better than you think. Let's hope that being married to your dad will have changed her and that being happy will make her treat you well."

He looked up at her then, his brown eyes big with tears. Sally's heart ached for him, for the pain he was obviously feeling.

"I hope so, Aunty Sally. I was so happy when dad told me we were going home but then finding Aunty Marjorie there was a real shock to me. John is ok about it; she likes him. But I don't think she will ever like me, Auntie. Why couldn't it be you? Why couldn't you have met my daddy and married him? I really want you to be my mum. And I want Granddad Jim and Granny Mo to be my granddad and grandma. You are my family, not her. I don't want to live with her! I would rather stay at Beaumont House!"

"You don't mean that Davey do you? Don't you want to be with your dad again? It would be good to be a proper family living in a house with a mum and dad and John, don't you think?"

"I do want that, but I don't want to live with HER! She doesn't want me either; she is only putting up with me because she has to. But I suppose I will be okay; I'm a big boy now, I can look after myself."

"That's my boy!" Sally hugged him. Then he burst into tears.

"Why, what's up with my lad? Davey - what's the matter?"

"I don't want to go to them! I will never see you again will I? Or Granddad Jim and Granny Mo? I want to be with you!" he sobbed and Sally's heart got even heavier. Yet again she held him as she had earlier in the day. She sat in the chair with him on her lap and he hid his face in her chest and she stroked his hair as she had so many times before. At times like this, all sorts of irrelevances go through the mind and she reflected how big he was now; he had grown so much during the almost four years since she had first seen him. Now his feet came much closer to the floor when he sat on her lap; she thought she soon wouldn't be able to hold him like this because he would be too big before long.....then realised this would probably be the last time she would hold him anyway. As she held him, her own tears were streaming down her cheeks at the thought that she would likely never see him again.

Eventually, Davey stopped crying but they stayed cuddled together in the chair for quite a while, each drawing comfort from the other. Sally reflected on her own unstable marriage and found herself wishing that she had, indeed, been the one to meet and marry Tony Adams; it couldn't be worse than what she had already! And then she would be Davey and John's mother. But of course, things were as they were. She glanced up at the clock. It was seven o'clock.

"My goodness!" she exclaimed. "Look at the time; we have to get you back to Beaumont House!" Davey sat up. "Go and find Granddad Jim, Davey. I will get Jess fed before we go."

Davey went off into the other room and Sally followed. Her mum was cuddling Jess, who was just stirring as it was feed time. Sally took the baby off her mum and went into the bedroom that used to be her room and settled down to feed Jess. The baby fed well and Sally changed her nappy, deftly folding the terry square to fit the baby's tiny bottom and expertly fixing the pin. Over the terry nappy went the plastic pants and then the clothes adjusted and she was wrapped up in her shawl again ready for the carry cot. When Sally went into the room where the others were her heart contracted to see Davey sitting cosily in the fold of her father's arm, cuddled against him whilst they watched the television.

"Right, we are ready!" she announced and the other three got up and got moving. No one spoke much in the car as they drove back to Beaumont House, but later, when they were in the house; they each hugged Davey and kissed him.

"Be a good boy now," said Granddad Jim. "Do your best lad. You will be all right. You're our big boy. And if you ever need us, we will always be there for you."

"Granddad is right Davey," said Maureen as she kissed him and hugged him. "We will always be there if you need us. Sally is going to give you our phone number and if you ever need to call us, you just go to a phone box and tell the operator you want to reverse the charges. Can you remember that?" She looked at him. "Well, anyway, we have put that down on the paper with the number. Remember that we love you and will never forget you and will think about you always."

Sally went with Davey to his bedroom. John was downstairs with the other children. She gave Davey a piece of paper.

"Now, Davey my love, keep this in a safe place. It is my address and Grandma and granddad's phone number and the instructions on how to reverse the charges. If things get bad, if you need us, phone them or come to me if you are able. Remember that you are not alone; we are here. And we will come if you need us. I love you Davey; I will never forget you, I have your little tiger on my shelf where I can see him every day. I will look at him and think of you and pray for you, my darling boy. I hope that you will never need to because I hope that you will be happy and grow up happy. Perhaps you will forget about us because you are happy and that's ok. Do you understand, Davey?"

He looked at her solemnly and nodded.

"Good boy. Now, give me a hug and I must go."

He put his arms around her and she leaned forward a little in order to hold him close for a moment, then she let him go, bent down to kiss his cheek. He flung his arms around her neck and she held him again.

"Be brave, my darling. I love you."

"I love you too, Aunty Sally,"

"Of course you do! I know that. Come on now, let's go and find Aunty Jean."

Sally looked up and saw Jean standing in the doorway, a look of deep sympathy on her face.

"Ah, here she is! I'm so sorry we are late back Aunty Jean, we quite forgot the time!"

Jean stepped forward and put a hand on Davey's shoulder.

"That's quite all right, Aunty Sally. Now then Davey, I think you'd better go get your wash and clean your teeth. John will be here in a moment because it is bedtime."

Davey went off and Sally heaved a sigh.

"Are you all right Sally?" asked Jean

"No, not really, Jean," was the reply, "truth, is, I'm really worried about him. I have given him a paper with my address and my parents' phone number on it. I want him to take it with him when he goes on Monday. Would you make sure he has it please? Of course, I don't want anyone else to know about it. But we had to give him a safety net to comfort him."

"Good thinking! Yes, I will make sure he has it," assured Jean.

"Thank you, Jean. Well, I'd better be getting home; my husband will think I'm lost!"

Sally returned downstairs to find Emily talking with her parents.

"Ah, Sally! I've been hearing that you had a good time with Davey. I'm sure you are aware that I am very worried about this situation but am hoping for a miracle." Emily said wryly.

"Yes, that makes four of us," replied Sally.

"Are you all right, my dear?" enquired Emily kindly.

"Well, apart from being worried about Davey and being heartbroken that I won't see him again, I'm ok..." Sally was dismayed to feel tears beginning to well up in her eyes and she turned away quickly. "We had better get going; Evan won't be pleased that I've been out so long."

They walked to the door and bade goodnight to Emily, got into the car and drove to Sally's house. It was obvious Evan wasn't there for it was all in darkness. Sally breathed a sigh of relief that he was out; she hadn't to say anything more about Davey. Her heart was heavy as she got her baby into bed and made herself a cup of hot chocolate to have while she watched some television before she retired for the night.

Chapter 14

A New Life

Davey wished with everything he had that Monday would never come. But of course it did. It came quite slowly; for Davey lay awake a long time on Sunday night. Everything was going through and through his head; he wanted to live with dad again, he loved his dad. But he feared what it would be like to live with Marjorie as his mother; there would be no Aunty Emily to protect him if she decided to punish him for something. And if there was no one to stop her, what could she end up doing to him? And, even worse than that, he was never going to see his beloved Aunty Sally again, nor Granddad Jim and Granny Mo. Davey was a brave little boy, but as he lay there in the dark, the tears trickled down onto his pillow when he thought of his lovely Aunty Sally. Would she forget about him? After all, she had her own baby to love now.

He awoke on Monday morning feeling very bad; he had a headache through crying and not sleeping. Aunty Jean came into his room and, taking one look at his face, knew exactly what sort of night he had had.

"Davey, lad, go and get washed and get yourself down to breakfast. You will not be going to school today of course. John! Get on! Have you washed yet?"

"No Aunty," replied John. He was very happy - today he was going home to live with daddy again! "Isn't it exciting, Aunty Jean? We're going home today!"

"Yes, I know, love. Go on – hurry up or you will miss breakfast."

John ran off to the bathroom. Davey followed more slowly. Jean looked after him, her heart aching for him. She busied herself taking their clothes out of the drawers and laying them ready for packing. There were some things that needed to come from the laundry but there was plenty of time; they were not coming for the boys until eleven.

Not long later, seated around the table in the Dining Room family room, Jean and her assistant Mary were presiding over breakfast. Jean noticed that John was happily stuffing his food down in his usual manner but Davey was picking at his food. The child had not been eating well ever since he knew about Marjorie being his stepmother; he was beginning to look pinched and thin. Jean fervently hoped that their fears would be ungrounded and that the boys would be well cared for by Marjorie.

Later, it was fairly quiet at Beaumont House. The children had gone to school and the younger children were being watched over in the nursery by Mary and Andrea. John was in there too, playing with the little ones but Davey was sitting alone in his family room, looking listlessly through a comic. His heart jumped into his throat when he heard the doorbell reverberate through the house. He went to the window and sure enough, there was his dad's car parked on the drive, along with another car, which he knew belonged to the Child Care officer, Miss Mason.

He went back to his chair and just sat and waited. This was IT. In a few minutes he would get into his father's car and leave Beaumont House for ever and go to – what?

The door opened, and in came Aunty Emily, followed by his father.

"Davey!" he heard his father say his name and he got up and walked towards him. His dad put his hand on his shoulder.

"All right son? Are you ready to go?"

Davey felt he would never be ready, but he nodded his head. They walked out of the room and in the hallway was John waiting with Aunty Jean and Miss Mason. Aunty Jean held a bag, which she handed to Tony Adams.

"Here are their clothes and things, Mr. Adams," she said.

"Thank you."

He turned to Aunty Emily.

"Thank you for taking such wonderful care of my boys over this past four years Mrs Brown. Please thank all the aunties for me."

Emily smiled warmly. She really liked this man; she fervently hoped things would work well, she was sure he deserved it, as did his sons.

"I will Mr. Adams. I hope you will bring the boys to see us sometimes."

"Yes, that would be very nice. Thank you," He turned towards the boys. "Are you ready lads? Then let's go! Your new mother is waiting for us at home. Miss Mason?" He turned towards the Child Care Officer. "Are you coming with us?"

"No, Mr Adams, not now. I think it's best I let you get the boys settled and I will come and visit you all in a few days," Miss Mason smiled and held out her hand to him. "I wish you all well."

Tony shook her hand. "Thank you very much. I am very happy; things are looking very good for us now. Goodbye then, Miss Mason, we will see you in a few days."

He turned to Emily.

"Goodbye then, Mrs. Brown,"

"I will see you out," Emily walked them to the door, then said goodbye to John and Davey. She hugged them both briefly, and then watched as they climbed into their father's car and he put the bag into the boot, got into the car and drove slowly down the drive. She waved at the car and saw three hands raised in waves before they had gone. Miss Mason's car followed. Emily shut the door.

"Please God," she prayed, "Let them be all right, let Davey be safe."

She went into her office, shut the door and went to deal with her paperwork.

****

The ride in the car seemed to take no time at all to Davey, who didn't want to arrive. But there was the house and dad ushered them out of the car and opened the front door for them.

"Marjorie!" he called, "We are here!"

Marjorie hurried down the stairs and immediately went to John and Davey. She hugged John first, who hugged her back joyfully, and then she hugged Davey, who held himself a bit stiffly. She looked at Tony, but he didn't seem to notice as he was looking towards the kitchen. He sniffed appreciatively.

"Mmm, something smells good!"

"It's cottage pie," she smiled up at him affectionately. "It will be ready soon. You go take your things upstairs, boys, then come down and we will have a drink together to tide us over until dinner is ready."

The boys ran off upstairs and Tony put his arm around his wife and kissed her.

"I appreciate you doing all this for me and my boys," he said.

Before long, they were all sitting in the kitchen with drinks of milk for the boys and tea for the adults.

"This afternoon, lads, we are going to take you to see the school that you will be going to. Of course you will only be going there for just over a term, Davey because next September you will go up to the secondary school. I hope you will be able to cope with two new schools in one year, son," Tony looked at his son anxiously.

"I will be okay, dad," Davey replied. He felt that two new schools was going to be nothing compared to what he might have to live with at home but of course he kept his thoughts to himself.

****

Two months had gone by and Davey started to relax. It seemed his fears had been ungrounded. Life wasn't bad really. Marjorie seemed to be making lots of effort to make things pleasant for everyone and she was a great cook! She seemed much softer now than she had been at the home and there was no doubt that his dad loved her very much. If he was alone with Marjorie, they were a bit quiet with each other; he felt she knew he didn't trust her. He tried to make sure he wasn't alone with her too often.

His dad appeared to be very happy; he was working locally most of the time and if he had to go away, he was only gone for a very short time. He said he just couldn't bear to be away from his family now they were all together again. He had told his bosses at work that he wanted local work and no work abroad. He needed to make things work with his family and he had good bosses who understood and did their best to make sure he stayed at home.

The weeks went by and the summer holidays were getting near. Davey had enjoyed his new school and was quite looking forward to going to the senior school. He had made some good friends and they went round to the local park to play football together. Yes, life wasn't bad after all.....

Catherine Mason had been to see them a few times over the three months they had been home and was relieved to see both the boys looking well and happy. She didn't have to, but she called Emily Brown after her third visit to report to her that things seemed to be going very well. She knew Emily would be glad to know, which she was. Catherine decided that she didn't need to visit them again.

Tony and Marjorie took the boys on holiday to South Wales during the summer break. Davey and John were very excited to be by the seaside. They had been to the seaside with Beaumont House and they had always enjoyed it. It was different being with dad and Marjorie; they did all kinds of things together. Dad played with them in the water whilst Marjorie enjoyed relaxing up the beach with a book. But she always made sure they had good things to eat in their picnics. Camping was fun; sleeping in tents and cooking over a camp fire was something the boys had not experienced before. Although they did eat quite a lot in cafes and chip shops. The Gower was beautiful; it had some lovely beaches and the weather was gorgeous; they needed nothing really except the sea and the sand. Sometimes they would play cricket on the beach and Marjorie would join in when they played.

Being on the Gower made Davey think about the day he had spent at the remote beach with Aunty Sally, Evan, Belinda and Juanita. He thought about the little house on the beach and wondered if they might go there one day. However, he couldn't remember what the beach had been called (he thought it had sounded something like 'false teeth', for some reason) and he had no idea where it was. He also remembered about the fair and he felt a big pang in his insides because it made him think about Aunty Sally. But it seemed that what she had said about Aunty Marjorie being kinder now she was married might be right.

The rest of the summer holidays passed well enough; Davey was out a lot with his friends playing football and other games in the park nearby. Sometimes he took John with him. They also visited Marjorie's parents, who John already called Nana and grandpa. Davey loved them too; they were not Granny Mo and Granddad Jim, it was true, no one would ever be like Granddad Jim to Davey, but grandpa Will and Nana Margaret were very kind to him and he liked being with them.

When the time came for him to start his new school, he went off on his first day, resplendent in his new school uniform. He was nervous, because the school was very much larger than what he was used to, but he found he was in a form with some of his friends, so together they discovered the school and got to know where everywhere was. It was hard getting used to having a different teacher for every subject; not only that but having to go to a different room for every lesson, but gradually he got used to it. He found that he could do the work quite easily and he had playtime with his mates.

One day, he came home from school to find Marjorie in his room. She was holding a piece of paper. His heart went into his mouth because he immediately realised what it was.

"What's this?" she demanded.

"It is Aunty Sally's address and Granddad Jim's phone number," Davey always told the truth.

"Well, you don't need this now," Marjorie deliberately ripped the paper into several pieces and Davey watched dumbly. For the first time since about June, he felt a sense of unease... He pushed the feeling away; after all, things had been all right hadn't they? His dad would always make sure he was ok. She went downstairs, the torn pieces still in her hand. Davey changed his clothes and sat down to do his homework.

Chapter 15

The Bad Times Begin

The change was so gradual that even Davey didn't notice it right away.

The family really enjoyed their first Christmas together. Tony and Marjorie pulled out all the stops to make sure they had a really good time. There were quite a few presents for each boy round the tree and there was a wonderful Christmas dinner cooked by Marjorie and they were joined by Marjorie's parents, Grandpa Bill and Nana Margaret. Dinner was a bit late because they all went to church together at St. Peter's Church. It seemed magical to Davey and John because they had never attended a Christmas service before. There were candles and choirboys and there was a crib scene with the baby Jesus surrounded by shepherds, kings, angels, sheep and donkeys. The music seemed like heavenly angels singing and it was lovely, all about peace on earth, goodwill towards men. Davey supposed that meant women and children too...

He thought about last Christmas and the ones before that when he had been at Beaumont House. There had only been one present, but he had enjoyed it, especially the last Christmas before Aunty Sally had been married. He wondered how she was and thought about baby Jessica; he thought she must be getting quite big now. He wondered if Auntie Sally even thought about him these days. And he wondered about Granddad Jim and Granny Mo, did they think about him?

They watched a film on television in the afternoon so that grandpa and nana could have a nap after their dinner, then they played a long game of Monopoly. Later they settled down to watch the Morecambe and Wise Christmas Show. While that was on, Marjorie put a buffet-style tea on the table so they could help themselves to food as they felt like it. The dinner had been so good that none of them really wanted to eat much but they enjoyed some light nibbles. Davey went to bed very happily that night; it was good to have had a real family Christmas.

When the boys had gone to bed, the adults sat around, having a drink and talking about things. They talked about Bob and his family; they had spoken to them over the phone earlier in the day to wish them a Happy Christmas. They were coming over to spend Boxing Day with grandpa and nana and Marjorie, Tony and the boys were going there too. They were looking forward to having a good day together. Then they got talking about Dickie. As usual, they had no idea where he was. Her parents were telling Tony a story about something Dickie had got up to when he was young.

The three of them were so engrossed in the story that none of them noticed that Marjorie fell silent. She found her thoughts taking her away to the days when they were all still living at home. There was a big age gap between Dickie and Marjorie. Bob was the eldest; Dickie was two years younger than him. Then Marjorie happened along when Dickie was ten. Margaret thought she wouldn't have any more children and the pregnancy came as a surprise to her and Bill.

As Marjorie's thoughts took her back, she found herself unwillingly remembering what she had suffered at Dickie's hands. He had done unspeakable things to her, things that a brother should never do to his sister, never mind one as small as she. It had started when she was only six. He was sixteen and he would threaten her that if she would tell he would really hurt her. She was so frightened and he did indeed hurt her many times. Her arms were often bruised with his finger marks where he twisted them. He threatened her and he bit her in places where it couldn't be seen.

She got very good at hiding things; she wouldn't let her mum bath her, saying she was a big girl and could do it herself. At school she would change very carefully for PE so that no one would see the bruises on her body. If she had bruises on her arms or legs she would pretend that she had forgotten to bring her PE kit and would have to sit writing out lines and sometimes she even got the cane for not having her kit so many times. But even having the cane was never as bad as what Dickie did to her. She hid the other signs too, stuffing her knickers right down in the washing basket, hoping her mother wouldn't see the blood...

He had left home when he was twenty, which was a big relief to Marjorie; she was free at last! She became much less withdrawn and started to make friends. Her parents noticed the difference in her and were relieved that she seemed to be coming out of her shell at last. They had never had any idea what had gone on.

As she sat and thought about these things; the hatred she had for Dickie rose to the surface again. And suddenly, she realised just why she never liked Davey.

There was something about Davey that reminded her of Dickie. Although she knew it wasn't Davey's fault at all, she started feeling against him again; it was unreasonable she knew, but somehow she just couldn't help it.

"Are you all right darling?" Tony's voice suddenly broke into her thoughts. She looked up, startled.

"Oh, er, yes. But I think I'm rather tired. It's been a very busy day."

"Of course you're tired, Marjorie dear!" her mother rose to her feet. "How inconsiderate we are! You've worked so hard today, making us that lovely dinner and tea. I didn't realise how late it had become. Come along, Bill dear, we must go – we have a busy day ourselves tomorrow."

Bill helped Margaret on with her coat and then slipped his own on. They kissed Marjorie and Tony goodnight and Tony saw them to the door. He locked the door behind them and went back into the sitting room.

"Thank you for all your hard work today, darling," he slipped his arm around her. "Come on, let's get to bed."

They went upstairs together and Marjorie was thankful to slip into bed and cuddle into Tony's arms.

****

One good thing that had happened over the course of time was that Davey and John were now much better friends. John was happy to be home with his dad and had stopped trying to get Davey into trouble. They did a lot of things together; they went out together to play football and they enjoyed playing in the garden or playing board games in one of their rooms. Davey was thankful that at last he didn't have to worry about John getting him into trouble.

For his part, John was sorry about what he had done to Davey during the Beaumont House years and was glad that Davey didn't seem to hold it against him. Now that Davey had gone up to the secondary school, he would tell John about what it was like. John was worried about going there next September.

"Don't worry John, I will help you and I will be there during playtimes so you can come to me if you need me," Davey comforted John when he expressed his worries about it. "It does seem a bit scary at first, but you soon get used to it. And you do some much more interesting things in science and other things like woodwork and metalwork."

John liked the sound of that, he was good with his hands and liked the idea that he could learn to make things.

****

"No Davey! You can't have another piece of cake!" Marjorie tapped his hand as he reached out for another piece. "I've noticed you are getting a bit tubby; we are going to have to cut down a bit on what you eat."

Davey looked at his father.

"Dad?" Davey appealed to Tony.

"Your mother is right, Davey," Tony admonished his son. "You are getting a bit tubby; you need to cut down a bit. Her cooking is just a bit too good isn't it?" Tony smiled fondly at his wife and she smiled back at him, then at Davey with a triumphant smile on her face. Davey didn't notice, he was looking down at his tummy which did, indeed, look bigger than it had been! Must have been all that yummy Christmassy food they'd had! He watched enviously as Marjorie cut another piece for John.

About a month after Christmas, Tony had to have a talk with Marjorie.

"Marj, I'm sorry love, but I have to go away to work for a while. It is over in Essex; I will have to stay there during the week but will come home at weekends. They said they have kept me at home as long as they could but now they need me to do this. Do you mind darling?" he asked anxiously, "Can you cope without me here during the week?"

"Of course I can! I'm used to looking after lots of children, remember? I did it for years. These two boys are no trouble anyway. But you promise you will be home every weekend?"

"I promise. I just couldn't do without you longer than five days at a time! Thank you for being so understanding darling."

Once Tony had gone to Essex, Marjorie made sure that Davey didn't overeat; in fact, he often wasn't given enough to eat. But if he asked for more, he was told sharply that he was too fat; his father had said so. And when he looked at her, she would look back at him in such a manner that it made his stomach churn over and remember Beaumont House days....

Gradually, Davey lost weight. The change was so gradual that his father, only home on weekends, did not notice. His clothes started to hang off him; he had problems keeping his trousers up. One day, he decided to say something to Marjorie.

"I am getting too thin, my trousers won't stay up. May I have some more food please?"

He gasped as the blow made his head reel, he was glad he was sitting down.

"How dare you? You certainly can't have any more food! You are too fat!" she screamed at him. John looked stunned as he sat and watched the scene.

"Go to your room!" Davey kept his head down and staggered out of the room. He went upstairs and lay down thankfully on his bed. Not long after, John came into the room. He stood by the bed.

"You all right Dave?" he asked. Davey nodded slightly.

"Yes. Don't worry. I think I will go to sleep now."

"Ok. But if you want me, I will come, just call me." John left the room. Davey felt sick, was it all going to happen again?

After that, Marjorie took every opportunity to punish Davey. She made him stay in his room a lot, telling him to do his homework. If he said he'd done it all, she would hit him. If he just came home with mud on his shoes, he got sent to his room. If he dared to answer her back over anything, she hit him. He stayed out of her way as much as possible, staying outside playing football or just walking the streets, anything to avoid going home. Often John was with him. It was affecting John because he could see that Davey was being badly treated and this time it wasn't his fault.

One day, Davey was so hungry that he actually stole a Mars bar from the local corner shop. Unfortunately, the owner saw him and called the police. They picked him up in a police car and gave him a good telling off. However, the policeman felt sorry for him, this boy looked so thin and pale; it was obvious that he was very hungry. They took him home. Marjorie was very polite and offered them a cup of tea and patted Davey on the head and told him it was ok, she still loved him. She told the police a story about how the boys were abandoned by their mother and she was still in the process of trying to rebuild their lives. They went away satisfied that she was doing a good job. Once they had gone, it was a different story. She went upstairs to his room and gave Davey the worst beating she had ever given him, using a shoe to hit him with as she screamed at him.

"How dare you do such a thing? Stealing is bad; I will not have you giving this family a bad name with your thieving. You – will – never- do – it- again." She hit him with every spaced-out word. "Do you understand?"

She looked at him cowering in front of her and suddenly she remembered herself after a beating from her brother. She flung down the shoe and rushed out of the room.

John crept into the room once she had gone and put his arms around Davey. They both sank to the floor and cried.

****

At school, they noticed that Davey was thin, pale and withdrawn. He had never been that big, but now he looked smaller. His form tutor kept him back after tutorial one day.

"Davey, is everything all right at home?"

He looked back at her for a moment, then lowered his head and nodded.

"Are you sure, Davey? You can tell me if there is anything wrong you know. You can trust me."

"It's fine, miss,"

"Ok. But you can come to me if you need help you know." She looked at the little boy before her with his head bowed, his clothes too big for him. She knew he was one of the youngest in her class; he seemed much too small to be at secondary school. She knew he lived with his father and stepmother and that he had been in a children's home for quite a while. She sighed. She just couldn't get rid of the feeling that things were just not right somewhere. But obviously he wasn't going to tell her anything.

"You may go, Davey."

"Thank you, miss." She watched as he slouched out of the classroom. She remembered when he had first come to this school; he had been just a normal little boy who had friends and enjoyed running around with a ball. Now he just sat quietly in class, only speaking when he was spoken to, never putting up his hand and volunteering. And, although he still had some friends, she never saw him smile.

Chapter 16

An Ending

If she had thought about it, Sally should have known it wouldn't last. But she was so busy looking after Jess that she didn't think. The change happened gradually; Evan started going to a snooker club with his mate and his mate's dad from next door. Sally was glad he had someone to go out with. And she reasoned that he wouldn't get into too much trouble playing snooker. He always came home at a reasonable time and things seemed fine. Then, he started coming home a bit later ('we were having a tournament') and one night he didn't come home until about three in the morning and he was very drunk. Sally knew then.

The row in the morning was fearful; Evan was sullen, Sally was upset. Jess was upset too - she couldn't understand what was going on. Sally knew he had been with a woman last night – who was she? And had it happened before with this one?

"I will never be enough for you will I?" she stated quietly. He didn't answer.

"I think you need to think about what you are doing, what you want, Evan," she said. "To my knowledge, this is the third woman you've had since we have been married – and that's only two and a half years! How many more will it be if we stay married? I know I had a problem when we first got married and that's why I overlooked the first one. But things have been so much better since we had Jess – or at least, I thought they were."

"They were, but somehow I can't seem to help it," he said, "Please forgive me Sally. I do love you and Jess."

"If I forgive you this time, how long will it be before it happens again? I just can't live like this, Evan. You have to decide what you want."

The following weeks were very difficult. Evan was morose and remote one time, then another time he was all over her, telling her he loved her and Jess and wanted to stay with them and asking her to give him another chance. Sally would just look at him and remind him that he had to choose; if he was going to stay with them he would have to not see any other women anymore. She knew he was having a hard time; he knew his own nature as she did. She doubted that he would be able to change his spots....

After another really late night, Evan came home, packed a bag and, after kissing the sleeping Jess, gazing at her with tears in his eyes, he looked at Sally and said "I'm sorry, Sally. You won't see me again."

And he was gone; just like that.

****

During the weeks that followed, Sally went through so many emotions. At first, she felt numb; she just couldn't believe that Evan had really gone and left her and their baby. Evan had always made so much of Jess that Sally could not understand how he could just walk away and never see her again. That is what he said he would do – he said he had thought it over and felt it would be kinder to Jess if he never had anything more to do with her; she wouldn't be subjected to the tug of war between separated parents.

He got paid on a Friday and he would post his wages envelope through the door late at night. She would lie in bed listening for the distinct sound of his car and rush down, wrench the door open and try to see him. He got wise to this after one night when she chased him down the road, shouting and crying and started leaving his car down the road so she wouldn't hear it.

Jim was absolutely furious with Evan and would often growl that if he ever got his hands on Sally's errant husband he would do something really nasty to him; Evan would regret what he'd done to their Sally. Maureen had to hush her husband lovingly but agreed that they had never liked Evan and hadn't been happy about Sally marrying him. Sally had known this; she wished she had followed her instinct and theirs and never went through with it. But at least she had Jess.

Sally didn't know how to feel; sometimes she was glad not to see him, at other times she was desperate to see him. She cried a great deal and it was a physical pain. Then she got really angry with him – how dare he do this to her and Jess! She thought back to the beginning, how reluctant she was and how insistent he had been; how determined that she was meant for him! She seethed with him and it carried her through the next few weeks...

She went to a solicitor to start the divorce proceedings. Not long after that she discovered that the mortgage was in arrears. It seemed that Evan had drawn all the money out of the joint account from which the mortgage was paid every month, thereby leaving nothing to pay with. Maureen and Jim paid the outstanding amount, for which she was deeply thankful and she made the arrangements with the mortgage company to take over the payments. Because Jess was very small, she signed up for Social Security and the money was taken care of. By this time, the Friday night envelopes had stopped appearing through the door. Money would be tight, but Sally was a good manager and they would cope.

Then the loneliness set in.

Jess was a delightful baby and Sally loved her so much and had lots of joy looking after her. They went often to spend time with her mum at Manvers, staying for tea when her dad came home and part of the evening until it was Jess's bedtime. Or her mum and dad came to visit them in Holly Avenue and they could stay with her after Jess was in bed. But she would have to come home after the visits, or her parents would go home eventually and the loneliness would feel more intense. Sally would be in her sitting room watching television, not really seeing it, praying that someone – anyone – would knock on the door. But no-one ever did.

Jess was different too. If she heard the front door open, or a noise outside, she would run to the door, arms open: "Dada!" Then she would realise that it wasn't her dad and she would turn away and it seemed to Sally that she physically drooped. Every time Sally saw it, she thought her heart would surely break.

Seeing Jess like this made her recall a day when she had walked into the dining room at Beaumont House and had seen Davey with his coat on, watching at one of the windows. He said his dad was coming, but he never did. John gave up long before Davey, who insisted on keeping his coat on until lunch time, persistent that his dad would come. In the end, Sally had led him gently away from the window and got him to take his coat off, saying that perhaps his dad had been called away on business or something. That was in the very early days of her time at Beaumont House, but she would never forget the desolate look on his face when he finally had to admit his dad wasn't coming; the same look she now saw on Jess's face.

Davey... She wondered how he was, how he was faring with Marjorie as his stepmother. Things must be all right, as she felt sure that Emily Matron would know if anything had gone wrong and would let her know. Marrying Tony Adams had been the making of Marjorie after all. Sally was glad that things had worked out for Marjorie and Davey, even if her own life had gone so drastically wrong. She also realised that, in spite of her efforts, she never did get to the bottom of why Marjorie had disliked Davey so much.

Chapter 17

Lost Hopes and Dreams

Sally was tiredly pushing the push-chair up the road. She had been in town shopping and now she had to walk home; it wouldn't take long, only half an hour or so. It seemed much longer though because it was mostly uphill and she was tired, and weary. She was so deep in thought; she never noticed a lorry stop beside her, until someone put a hand on her shoulder. She jumped violently.

"Sally!" a familiar voice, not heard for far too long, spoke her name. She turned to see the much thought-about dimpled cheeks and cute smile gazing down at her.

"Joe!" her heart leaped at the sight of him. Obviously, he looked older, he had lost his young man smooth cheeks and his hair had lightened in colour and was less dense, but he still looked very good to her.

"What are you doing here?"

"Ever since I heard about you and Evan splitting up I have been looking for you," he said. "I have driven my lorry up and down this road instead of going round the outskirts as I would normally do to get to my depot, in the hope I would see you," he explained. "I wanted to know how you are."

"Oh," Sally dropped her eyes. She had hoped for much more for a few moments. "I'm ok thanks. How are things with you?"

"Oh, fine.....I wonder, would you let me come and see you?" Joe searched her face anxiously. His heart lifted when he saw her smile.

"Yes, I'd like that very much."

His smile widened in delight; this was more than he dared hope.

"That's great! When would suit you? Obviously I can only come in the evening because I'm at work during the day."

"Any evening really; I can't go far because of my baby. I like her to have a regular bedtime routine."

"Okay, that's great. Must go now; I'm supposed to be working. I will see you very soon." Joyfully, Joe leaped back into his cab and drove off, giving her a cheerful wave as he pulled away.

Sally resumed her walk, rejuvenated somehow and she couldn't help smiling; she was very happy. Was something good actually going to happen to her at last?

****

All was quiet in Sally's house. Jess was in bed sleeping peacefully and Sally was sitting on her sofa, watching television and doing some hand sewing on the dress she was making. A knock came at the door. Sally went to answer it and her heart leaped when she saw it was Joe standing there.

"Oh! Why didn't you let me know you were coming?" she said, "Give me a chance to tidy myself up!"

Joe smiled. "You look very good to me," he said. She opened the door wider and stepped back so he could come in. He came in and she shut the door. She indicated towards the sitting room. He went through; she followed him.

"Do you want to take your jacket off?" she asked. He took it off and laid it on the back of the chair and then went to sit on the sofa. She sat down next to him. They looked at each other for a few moments. Sally smiled.

"It's so good to see you Joe," she said.

Joe traced his finger around her face, following the line of her cheekbones, caressing her gently. He leaned forward and kissed her lightly on her lips. She closed her eyes and sighed quietly. He kissed her again and she leaned into the kiss, which became more urgent. Then he stopped and looked at her.

"Oh Sally! I have longed to hold you in my arms again for simply ages," Joe whispered tenderly. "I hated Evan for taking you off me, for taking you away when I wanted you so badly."

Sally sank into the fold of his arms and rested her head on his chest.

"I was such a fool," she said, "I knew I had made a mistake as soon as I'd married him. I had one hell of a time with him, he just couldn't keep away from other women. I don't know why I married him; I should have stayed with you, we were so good together."

Joe lay back on the sofa and she lay down with him, her head on his chest still. It felt so right; just like coming home. She was where she should always have been. She wondered again what on earth she had been doing with Evan when she could have had Joe. But now she had been given another chance. Now she was free to love the way she wanted to. She put her hand under Joe's polo shirt and he drew in his breath. The looked at each other for what seemed like a long time and then he started to unbutton the top of her dress and slipped his hand inside. Sally's skin tingled at his touch and her whole being longed for him.

She was as beautiful as he had ever imagined her to be and Joe savoured every touch of her... for so many years he had wanted to do this; he couldn't believe he was here with her now; it was like a dream come true. She was so responsive as she gave herself to him unreservedly. As they lay entwined afterwards, spent and relaxed, they held each other close.

Sally gave a contented sigh – so this was what it was like to be really loved! How much she had missed! How lucky she was to have found it now.

****

The following couple of weeks were the happiest Sally had known for a long time. Joe spent as much time with her as he could. He formed the habit of coming straight from work in order to see Jess before Sally put her to bed. He played with her, delighting in her squeals of laughter as he teased and tickled her. He thought about that bastard Evan – how could he leave his sweet little daughter? He was coming to love her as he loved Sally – come to that, he couldn't understand how Evan could have left Sally. She was so loving and sweet and so giving to him. He loved being with his two princesses, as he thought of them. On the weekend, he went up to Manvers with them and was welcomed by Jim and Maureen. They were very pleased to see him again and it was lovely to be with them once more.

The more time he spent with them, the more awful he felt; however was he to tell Sally what he needed to tell her, what he must tell her? He kept putting it off. He felt sure she must suspect something, but she didn't seem to, even though sometimes he never stayed very long in the evenings. He always had a valid excuse – he had arranged to see a mate that evening, or he had to get home to help his mum to do something. He loved it when he could stay the night with her, sharing breakfast in the mornings with her, seeing her all tousled from sleep but still looking lovely. He loved sleeping wrapped around her.

He knew he could not put it off any longer. One evening, when they were downstairs and idly letting their hands wander over each other, he said:

"Sal, there is something I have to talk with you about."

She sat up and looked at him. He was looking very serious. As if in premonition, her heart became heavy.

"What is it, love?"

Joe sat up, straightened his clothes and said: "Sally, I should have told you this from the beginning, but I was so thrilled at being with you again, and, and, making love with you is something I've dreamed of ever since we met and I couldn't believe you would be willing so soon...."

"Yes?" Her eyes seemed to grow big and round as she looked at him. His heart nearly failed him – he didn't want to tell her....

"The thing is Sally – I am engaged to be married!"

"What? Who to? How long? When will you be married?" She sat up suddenly, the questions came spilling out

"Later on this year, first Saturday in September," he said quietly.

"Why didn't you tell me? Straight away?" she now had tears in her eyes. He could hardly bear it.

"I wanted you so badly....."

"In other words, you wanted me for sex!" Sally was angry now.

"No! It's not like that!"

"How is it like then?"

I've always wanted you, ever since I met you. And I hated Evan for taking you!"

"And you wanted to pay me back for leaving you?"

"Yes! No! I love making love with you!"

"It's sex again! What's the matter? Won't SHE sleep with you until you're married? Just like I wouldn't sleep with you, like I wouldn't sleep with Evan so he was determined to marry me?"

"No! Sally, listen!"

But Sally was beyond listening now.

"You were using me for sex! Using me to pay me back, to pay Evan back! You couldn't wait to jump into his bed! I suppose you thought it wouldn't matter now that I'm a divorced woman! Cheap, used goods! Get out!

"Sally, please..."

"No! Get OUT! GO! I never want to see you again! Get out of here – now!"

She was standing now, holding her clothes around her, angrily pointing at the door. Joe gathered his jacket and walked towards the door. He turned, tried to plead with her again, but she pushed him towards the front door, still shouting, "Go!"

He went through the door and she slammed it shut behind him. Then she went into the kitchen, sat at the table, put her head down on her arms and wept bitterly.

****

A couple of nights later, there was a knock on the door. Sally opened the door on the chain. It was Joe.

"Sally," he said, "will you let me explain?"

"You explained quite adequately the other night! Go away!" She shut the door in his face. Then she walked back into her living room, turning off all the lights in the hallway and shutting the living room door. She turned the TV on loud. If he knocked again, she would not hear.

But Sally was heart sore; she couldn't forget Joe. She kept thinking about the past fortnight when he had been there with her and Jess. She remembered how he had seemed to love Jess, loved playing with her and making her laugh. And how he seemed to just want to be with her; he hadn't wanted sex all the time had he? He had told her that he loved her. He had told her how he had watched out for her for so long, had worried about her when she was married to Evan and then when he heard the marriage had broken up, he worried about her again...

Perhaps she had been too hasty making him go away. He couldn't help being engaged could he? After all, he had been free to do what he wanted while she was struggling in her marriage.

Next day was Sunday, and Sally and Jess always went to have dinner and tea at Manvers with Jim and Maureen. She was glad of the diversion for a while.

Maureen, however, knew her daughter inside out and knew that things were not well with her.

"How's Joe?" she enquired, and was dismayed to see her daughter's face crumple. "Oh, what's happened?"

Sally told her about Joe's engagement and their row – of course, she never told about the sex part.

"I threw him out I was so angry! Then he came back on Friday night and tried to explain and I wouldn't let him. Oh mum, I wish I'd listened to him! This past couple of weeks I've had with him have been the best of my life so far. Maybe he might have changed his mind about getting married. Now I've sent him away and he will go and get married. Being married to Evan has just made me suspicious of everyone; I expect all men to be like him. But, deep down, I know that Joe isn't like him at all and now I've lost him! How could I be so stupid?" Sally was sobbing now and Maureen put her arms around her daughter, not knowing quite what to say.

Jim came in with Jess, having just been out in the garden to look at the ducks and moorhens on the ponds. He looked at his two women, then, seeing the signal from Maureen, he went back out again, talking cheerfully to Jess in his arms. He took her to look at the roses at the side of the house, all the time wondering what was wrong with his girl, but he knew his wife would tell him about it later. They didn't want Jess to see her mummy upset as it would make her cry too. After a little while, they went back in and Sally and Maureen were busily getting tea ready.

Later on, after he had dropped Sally and Jess back home, he asked his wife what it was all about. When she told him, he was thoughtful.

"I always liked Joe," he said. "He certainly did wrong in not telling Sally straight away but I think she definitely overreacted. I think Joe has always loved our Sally and I think he would have made it right if she had let him."

"I think so too," his wife replied. "Isn't there anything with can do Jim?"

"I don't see there is anything we can do. I can hardly go to Joe and persuade him not to marry his girl can I?"

Maureen shook her head.

"Looks like we are just going to have to leave it; we can't interfere. But I feel so sorry for Sally; she has been through so much these three years."

Jim clenched his fists.

"If I could just get my hands on that Evan......."

"Now Jim - you wouldn't! In any case, it wouldn't make things any better!" Maureen protested.

"It would make me feel better!" replied Jim grimly.

****

After that, whenever Sally walked up and down the road to and from the city, she kept her eyes open for the lorry that Joe drove. Every day, she looked and hoped, but the weeks went by with never a sight of him.

On the first Saturday of September, as Sally hung her washing out on the line, she heard on the wind the faint strain of church bells. Her heart was heavy – she wondered if they were the bells for Joe's wedding. She didn't know what time or where he was getting married. The bells seem to mock her; with every chime she felt more and more as if the heart was going out of her.

She hurriedly finished hanging her washing and ran inside, shutting her door so she couldn't hear the bells anymore. But it didn't make her feel any better. She knew for sure she had lost him now.

Chapter 18

A Change of Direction

Joe walked away from Sally's house despondently. He knew he had handled things so badly, letting her think it was sex he wanted from her. He loved Sally; he had always loved her, ever since she first gave him a chip. She was all he had ever wanted, truly wanted in his life. He thought he would never forget the evening when he saw Evan walking down the road towards him with his Sally. The bottom dropped out of his world that night when she had chosen to go with Evan.

When he realised that she was going out with Evan on a regular basis, he and Pete had gone to see her at Beaumont House one evening and had tried to talk to her about him. Evan had such a bad reputation; they just knew that he was so wrong for Sally. But she had refused to listen to them; Evan had really got to her and she was hooked. He could see that there was nothing he could do but leave her to her fate; he felt sure the outcome would not be good.

Sally and Evan had married about 9 months later and a few months later he heard she was pregnant; so perhaps things were going all right for her after all.

Not long after he heard about Sally's pregnancy, he met Liz in a pub. She was friendly and chatted to him and he allowed it; he didn't have much interest in women just now really, he was still hurting over Sally, still watching over her from afar. If that b***** hurt his girl, he would regret it!

He and Liz often met up, as if by accident in the pub after that, she doing her best to make it look as if it were unplanned – but in fact she went there every night hoping to see him. Before too long, they became a 'couple', he took her home to meet his mum. Gladys didn't like her; it wasn't long before privately, she nicknamed the girl 'the Harridan' – Gladys had her measure immediately! It was obvious the girl had set her sights on Joe.

After seeing Liz for a few months, Joe suddenly became aware that, apparently, he was going to marry her! He was sure he hadn't asked her, not even when he'd had too much to drink, which he did sometimes because he got rather depressed when he thought about Sally. He realised he had to let her go in his mind, and, if Liz wanted to marry him, he might just as well, because it was obvious that Sally was out of his reach. If he couldn't have Sally, he didn't much care who he ended up with. In his present state of mind, he never thought about the consequences of marrying someone he didn't love.

Then he heard that Evan had left Sally and their baby! In spite of his forthcoming marriage, once Joe heard about that it was all he could think of. He didn't know for sure where she lived but he knew the basic area. It was useful that he could go that way often in his work. He drove about for quite a few weeks and saw nothing of Sally. He almost gave up hope – until that wonderful day when he saw her. He stopped his lorry by her without any proper thought about what he was going to say. And he suddenly realised he was asking if he could see her...

On his way after he'd seen her, his conscience pricked him – what about Liz? He decided he wouldn't worry about that – he just had to see Sally!

It absolutely blew his mind that she made love with him on that first visit – it seemed incredible to him. When he was seeing her before, she would never let things get far in that respect. She was a decent girl; she had standards which he respected. He just loved being with her and with her parents too. It all seemed to be going so well before she met Evan the Rat. This time, she actually seemed to lead the way, made it clear she wanted him – and what man is going to turn away such an offer, especially when he is already besotted with her and had been for so very long? He realised now that he had come along just at the time when she was most vulnerable; needing reassurance that she could still be attractive to someone and also needed loving closeness to someone; her self-confidence had taken a severe battering and she had never been that confident anyway. She had always seemed delicate and vulnerable to him.

But it had made it very difficult to tell her about Liz. He had been with Liz quite a while and the wedding was not far away now. Liz wanted him, and what Liz wanted she got, apparently. Having met her parents, he realised that a while back. They refused her nothing, and when they realised she had her sights set on Joe, they backed her up one hundred percent.

Call him weak, but he couldn't help himself around Sally; the more he saw her, the more he had to see her. And that little Jess, she was beautiful too. He adored the baby and, in spite of the fact she was the child of the hated Evan, he loved her and wished she was his.

Gladys looked at her son with concern. He had not been himself for quite a while now. He was quiet; he hardly ate anything and was listless. She had only seen him like this once before – that was when that Sally threw him over almost 4 years ago. She had hated seeing him like that, knew he was hurting, but he was young then and young people go through these things...

"Joe my son," Gladys put her hand on his shoulder as he sat at the kitchen table one evening. He was just sitting there, cup of tea going cold in front of him, smoking yet another cigarette. He had always smoked but not usually as much as he was doing now, he was almost chain-smoking.

"Joe," she continued, "something is obviously bothering you a lot. Do you want to talk about it?"

"No," he pushed his chair back and stood up. "It's all right, don't worry mum."

"But I am worried son. I hate to see you so distracted. I haven't seen you like this since that Sally broke up with you over three years ago."

The mention of Sally broke his reserve. He sat down again and put his head in his hands. Gladys knew she had hit a chord.

"Oh son! Is it Sally again? Surely not - she's married isn't she?

"Well, she was, but she's not now. That creep Evan has left her and their baby," Joe said. "I saw her a couple of weeks ago in the street. I have been going to see her."

Gladys sank down on another kitchen chair.

"'You've been seeing her? Son – you're going to be married in a few weeks!"

"I know, I know!" he replied bitterly. "Oh mum, I love her so! I've always loved her, never stopped loving her all this time. And it suddenly seemed I had another chance with her. But now it's all gone wrong!"

"How has it gone wrong love?" Gladys asked gently.

"I know it was wrong, but I never told her about being engaged straight away. I know I should have told her, but it was so wonderful being with her again that I, well, I just kept putting off telling her. I did tell her at last and she was so angry with me and she threw me out! I did try to go back a couple of nights later to explain, but she wouldn't let me."

Gladys' heart ached for her son. He had always been so good to her, she so wanted him to be happy. She knew he would never be happy with the Harridan.

"What do you want to do son?"

He looked at her.

"I was so confused mum," he said, "There I was going along with this marriage thing, and then I heard about Sally and Evan splitting up. That was all I could think about. Then, when I saw her, I knew I had to see her, had to have another go. But there is Liz – what shall I do mum? You know I hate to hurt anyone and Liz is so set on me. And Sally doesn't want to know me anymore. If she'd only given me a chance I would have told her I was going to break off my engagement. Now I don't know what to do."

"Well dear," she said carefully, "You know I've never tried to interfere in your life and have never given you any unwanted advice. But since you ask, I think you should be asking yourself if you really love Liz. Do you think you will be happy with her? I think you've just been going along with it because you didn't care. "

Joe looked at her thoughtfully as she carried on:

"Last time you lost Sally, I knew that you were hurting badly, but you were so young then, only just 18 and I felt perhaps it was best not to say anything. But this time, as you said, it seems as though you have been given a second chance. And anyone blessed with a second chance should never waste it! The first time you gave in too easily. But now you're older and a man. Are you going to give in easily this time? Surely this girl is worth fighting for?"

"But she said she didn't want to see me again! And Liz will be very upset if I break up with her!"

"Believe me son, Liz will survive! She's a very forceful young lady and she won't give you up easily, but if you truly love Sally, you will be doing Liz an injustice marrying her - because you will never be able to give the relationship everything. And it's better to break up before the marriage rather than suffer and break up a marriage when perhaps children might be involved."

"I think that I have some serious things to think about. I have drifted along with Liz's plans to get married because it seemed the easiest thing to do. But now that I've seen Sally again, I realise that I don't think I love Liz enough to carry on with it, no matter whether I have Sally or not." Joe was thoughtful. His mother had really made him think properly for the first time since he met Liz. Perhaps she was right – and marriage was a big commitment. He knew that if he married Liz he would be faithful no matter what, but what might the cost be? If he could be so easily distracted from Liz just by meeting Sally again, did he really love her enough to commit his life to her?

"I think I'll go for a walk mum," he got up again. "See if it will clear my head a bit."

Gladys sat on at the table, feeling the draught as he opened the door and staring after him as the door shut. She hoped she had said the right things and that he would make the right decisions.

The next evening, Joe was sitting in the living room in Liz's house with her. Her parents were out and yet again, Liz wanted to discuss the wedding. He listened to her prattling on about what decorations she wanted on the tables and what sort of crockery etc. she wanted. His mind just wasn't on it somehow – all he could think about was Sally and her baby Jess. The longer he was away from Sally, the more he wanted to see her. He thought about the softness of her hair, the smoothness of her cheeks, the way her eyes sparkled when she smiled. Sally's smile was so spontaneous, always so genuine. Liz's smile, in comparison, was tight and the smile often never reached her eyes...

"I'm sorry Liz," he suddenly heard his own voice. She never even noticed; she went on talking.

"Liz!"

She noticed then.

"What is it?" she was impatient. "We have to get this sorted."

"No we don't."

"What? Of course we do!"

"No, we don't because it's not going to happen."

"What are you talking about?" he had Liz's attention now.

"I'm talking about this wedding. It's not going to happen Liz. I'm not going to marry you!"

Liz looked at him as if he was mad.

"Of course it's going to happen! The date is set, the invitations are sent out! I have my dress, the bridesmaids have theirs."

"No Liz, it's not going to happen. It will have to be cancelled. I'm not going ahead with it."

"But Joe!" she wailed, "why not?"

"I am not going to marry you because I don't love you. I'm fond of you, but I don't love you. I love someone else; have always loved her, for several years now. I would be doing you an injustice to marry you when I love someone else. I'm sorry."

Liz just couldn't believe what she was hearing. All her careful plans were falling about her ears!

"But you asked me to marry you!"

"No, I didn't. You decided we were going to marry and I just went along with it. But I realise now that I'm very wrong for doing that. I don't want to marry you Liz. I don't want to spend my life with you. I'm sorry if I have hurt you, but I just can't do it."

"But Joe - I love you. And you love me, even if you think you don't!" Liz was crying now.

Joe was finding this very difficult; he couldn't stand it when women cried. Liz knew this and was hoping it would change his mind....

"I'm sorry Liz. I'm going now and I won't be seeing you again."

"No!" the tears stopped very suddenly. She was angry now. "You will not walk out on me! The wedding will go ahead!"

"Then it will go ahead without me," he replied quietly. "Goodbye Liz. I hope you find someone else more worthy of you."

Joe got up and walked out, shutting the door firmly behind him. Liz sat and stared after him. She was so angry! He had done her out of her dream wedding!

As Joe walked down the road from Liz's house, he felt like a weight had been lifted off his shoulders. He couldn't figure how he had come to let himself get involved that far with Liz in the first place! He could see that she wasn't really a terribly nice girl, not like his Sally......

His Sally! But she wasn't his Sally was she? He wondered what he was going to do about that. He wasn't to know that Fate had it all in hand – but in such a way Joe could never have foreseen it.

Chapter 19

Suspicion

Catherine Mason was meeting with Emily at Beaumont House. She had brought a child into care that morning; an emergency admittance. They had completed the necessary paperwork and Catherine stood up to leave. As Emily showed her to the front door, she asked if Catherine had seen the Adams boys lately.

"No, I haven't. But it's strange that you have asked that because a memo appeared on my desk just this morning. Apparently, a teacher at the secondary school where the older boy goes is concerned about him. I will have to do a follow up."

"Did it say what concerns they have?" Emily's forehead wrinkled as she frowned.

"No, it wasn't at all specific. And I don't know when I will be able to see the teacher; I have so much work on right now! The city seems to be going mad; I'm being called on left, right and centre. We all are, all the social workers are rushed off their feet."

"Well, do your best."

"I will, although I must say that they seemed fine the last time I saw them."

"But that was well over a year ago! And of course things were going to be ok when they knew you were likely to be calling."

"Yes, I suppose you are right. Well, I will see what I can do. Goodbye for now Mrs Brown. And I do hope young Sarah will settle quickly."

"I'm sure she will. Lillian is a very caring housemother. She will look after Sarah."

"Thank you." Catherine stepped over the threshold and walked to her car. Emily shut the door, thinking about Davey. Would that child never have a happy life?

****

Tony Adams continued to work in Essex all through the summer holidays. When he was home at weekends he was so taken up with Marjorie and her with him. He barely noticed that Davey was either out or in his room nearly all the time. Although he did mention that Davey was very silent these days.

"Oh well darling, you know what boys are like! He is twelve now and is on the threshold of being a teenager. They can turn into such strange beings; you never quite know what they are going to be like. Davey has started a bit early, that's all."

"Oh yes, you are probably right my love. I was a horrible teenager; I could hardly bring myself to talk with any adults, especially my parents."

"There you are then!" Marjorie snuggled next to him on the sofa, her feet tucked up under her. "So, how long will you be working in Essex? Are we going to get a holiday this year?"

"Just a few weeks more, my love; the boss says when it's finished I can have a couple of weeks off. We will take the boys out of school and go away somewhere."

"Oh, that will be very good. I can hardly wait. I shall be so glad when you are home all the time."

"Mmm. Me too... fancy an early night?" he ran his finger around her breast. She laughed and unfolded herself, got up and put out her hand to pull him up. He caught hold of her hand and pulled her towards him. She landed on him with a shriek of laughter and he turned her round to lay her on the settee and kissed her thoroughly.

Davey heard the laughter as he lay in bed. Although he was glad his dad was happy, he wished he could have found someone else to be happy with. He remembered when he was at Beaumont House wondering when the nightmare would end. Aunty Sally came along and made the nightmares a lot less.

For a while things here seemed to get much better. Then suddenly, around Christmas time his stepmother seemed to lose it and took every opportunity to punish him, slapping him for very little, making him go hungry, often not letting him eat at all, sending him up to his room and occasionally going really mad and beating him with anything she could lay hands on. Davey wondered how much more he could take. He lay in bed and tried to plan how he would run away and find Aunty Sally. She would comfort him and let him live with her... Davey let his thoughts dwell around Sally until he fell asleep.

****

September came and John started at the secondary school and went along with Davey. It was good for them to have each other to go to school with. John felt much more confident having Davey with him. Davey's form tutor happened to see them together and couldn't help comparing them to each other. John looked well-built and healthy with a good colour in his face. Davey was just the opposite. In fact, she thought he looked even worse than the last time she had seen him; he seemed to have shrunk somehow, and walked with a sort of droop, with his head down as if trying to hide himself away.

As it happened, she knew that a Child Care officer was coming to see her after school hours that evening; she wondered just what she could tell her. Davey had consistently refused to tell her anything so she only had her gut feelings to go on.

****

Miss Mason walked away from the school in a thoughtful frame of mind. The teacher, Mrs Webb, couldn't tell her anything concrete, just the observations she had made. She had said that Davey said there was nothing wrong but she remembered what he had looked like when he first came to the school a year ago and what he was like now. It strongly indicated to her that something was very wrong. Mrs. Webb had been a teacher for quite a few years and was adept at knowing her pupils and noticing when things weren't right.

Catherine decided that she needed to go to the family home right away, which she did. Marjorie answered the door and was surprised to see the child care officer standing there.

"Oh! Miss Mason; I did not expect to see you. Is there something wrong?"

"No, not at all Mrs Adams. I was in the area on other business and decided to call and see how things are."

"Would you like to come in?" Marjorie held the door open and Catherine stepped inside. "Would you like a cup of tea?"

Catherine said she would and sat down in the warm and homely kitchen. John came in and said hello shyly.

"Hello John," Catherine said warmly. "How are you getting on?"

"John has started at the secondary school now," Marjorie told her proudly. "I can hardly believe he is old enough! I have known him since he was five."

"Is that so John? And are you enjoying being there?"

John nodded.

"Yes it is good. And Davey looks after me at playtimes and has dinner with me."

"How is Davey?" Catherine looked around as if she expected him to materialize in front of her.

"He is fine," Marjorie told her. "He is out playing football. He is always out. Only in for meals – you know what boys are like!"

"I do indeed. Well, I had better go, it is getting late and I have a lot of paperwork waiting for me in the office. Thank you for the tea."

Catherine got up and Marjorie went with her to the door.

"How is your husband?" Catherine spoke just as she was in the process of stepping through the door.

"Oh, he is fine. He is working away at the moment and is only home at weekends. But soon he will be home all the time again and we will be having a holiday all together. We are all looking forward to it."

"I'm sure. It must be hard having him away so much."

"We manage." Marjorie said sharply. "Well, goodbye Miss Mason, thank you for dropping in on us."

She shut the door and went into the sitting room to watch Miss Mason's car drive away from behind the net curtains.

"Davey!" she stood at the bottom of the stairs and called loudly. "Come down here at once!"

Davey appeared at the top of the stairs and made his way slowly down. He had seen the Child Care Officer arrive from his bedroom window and had deliberately stayed out of the way.

When he was within reach, she hit him around the head.

"Who have you been talking to?"

"No one."

"You're lying. Tell me! She didn't come round just because she was being friendly. You have been talking to someone. Who is it? Your teacher?"

"No! No, I've said nuffink to no-one, honest!"

"I don't believe you. You have always been a liar." She hit him over and over until he managed to wrench himself away and ran back up to his room and locked the door behind him. She shouted for him to come back down but he ignored her. In the end she gave up. He had no tears; he had long since given up crying because it did no good. The pain was too bad. He put his pyjamas on and climbed into bed, he knew it would be yet another time when he would go hungry. He eased his bruised and aching body into a slightly more comfortable position, if that was possible, and allowed his thoughts to weave around a fantasy meeting with Sally when she would see immediately that he was being hurt and take him home to live with her.

Chapter 20

Home is a Dangerous Place

It was the Saturday before Tony Adams was due to finish in Essex. He and Marjorie were talking over their plans to take the boys away the following weekend. John and Davey were both out with their friends as it was a lovely day, even though it was the end of September. They were startled when a loud knock came at the front door. Tony went to answer it. Marjorie stiffened when she immediately recognised the voice that spoke to Tony. She turned towards the door as Tony walked through into the kitchen, followed by her brother Dickie.

"Marjorie! Look who is here!" Tony sounded pleased, thinking that she would be happy to see Dickie.

Dickie went up to Marjorie and planted a smacking kiss on her cheek. "Hello Sis! Aren't you pleased to see me then?" He laughed. Marjorie mentally gathered herself together.

"Oh, er, of course - I was just surprised that's all. You never let us know you were coming."

"I just decided on a whim, old girl. I was between jobs and thought, 'why not go and see the old man and woman and my delightful sister and her new family?' So here I am."

"Well, don't just stand there! Sit down. We were just having a coffee. Would you like one?" Tony indicated a chair at the table and Dickie pulled out the chair and sat down. He nodded.

"Yes please, that sounds good."

Marjorie put a mug of coffee in front of him and then sat the other side of Tony, as far away from Dickie as she could round the table. What did he want? Why was he here? She sat and listened as the two men talked. It was obvious that Tony liked the other man and they soon found subjects of mutual interest; sports, football in particular and fishing. Tony told Dickie about his work and that he was actually working away right now but would be finishing at the end of the week.

"Marjorie gets lonely when I'm not here, so we will both be glad when next weekend comes, won't we, dear?" Tony turned to her fondly and she managed a smile for him.

"Well," said Dickie heartily, "she won't be lonely this week; I'll come round and keep her company."

"That will be really great! I'm sure she will love that; you two haven't seen each other for a long time so I'm sure you must have lots to talk about. And you will be able to get to know the boys too."

"Oh yes, I am looking forward to getting to know the boys. I haven't seen them yet because they weren't at the wedding were they?"

"No, they weren't there. But we are a very happy little family now, aren't we my love? And it's all down to this very special sister of yours!" Tony planted a kiss on the top of her head as he stood up and collected the mugs.

"Well, I must get on with dinner as the boys will be coming home very soon for food. You know what boys are like – bottomless pits!" to her own ears, Marjorie's laugh sounded hollow, but the men didn't seem to notice.

"How about you and me going to the playing field to see if the boys are there?" suggested Tony to Dickie. "I'm sure Marj would prefer to have the kitchen to herself while she performs her magic on the food; you will have some dinner with us won't you? Come on, if we are lucky, we might get a game of footie."

"Good idea," Dickie immediately rose to his feet and followed Tony towards the back door.

"We will see you later darling." Tony nuzzled her neck for a moment as she stood at the sink with potatoes in her hands.

When they had gone, she sank onto a chair and put her head in her hands. Why did he have to come and spoil things? Would she never get over the way she felt? Would she never be able to block out the fear that always stabbed at her whenever he was near? She remembered the pain, the dreadful fear, the blood...Oh God! Why, why?

****

Although he was staying with their parents, Dickie spent most of Saturday with them and a great deal of Sunday too. In fact, she invited her parents over for Sunday dinner and they came. On the surface, everything was fine. As long as there were plenty of people around, Marjorie felt reasonably safe.

On Sunday evening, when Tony was about to set off on his drive back to Essex, she clung to him.

"What's this?" he murmured into her hair.

"Do you have to go? I wish you wouldn't go!" she was tearful

"Oh darling, you know I hate to go, but it's only this one week now. I won't be back until Saturday morning because there will be a completion celebration meal which I will have to attend on Friday evening, but I promise I will be home as early as I can."

"Please get here as soon as you can," she pleaded tearfully.

"I will," he promised, "and in the meantime you will have Dickie for company sometimes during the week. The time will soon pass."

"But that's the problem; Dickie is the problem. I don't want him here, we never got on. He upsets me."

"Oh darling, don't be silly – he's your brother! And you are adults now; it's not the same as when you were young and living at home. Nearly every brother and sister fight you know."

"Yes, I guess you are right. I'll see you next weekend then. I love you. Drive safely." She kissed him goodbye and stood on the step and waved as he drove away.

She knew she could never tell him the real reason why she didn't want Dickie around – that he had sexually abused her for four years. She knew it was her fault; Dickie had told her that it was. It was her fault because she was so pretty and had beautiful hair. She had once got some scissors and cut off all her hair in great clumps. She had got into lots of trouble with her mother for it, but she never told her why because she knew Dickie would punish her, he would beat her, burn her with his cigarettes and she would deserve it.

As she sat watching television she was startled when the door of the sitting room opened and in walked Dickie with a bag.

"What do you want?" she was hostile.

"Oh now, there's a way to speak to your loving brother!" his eyes were mocking. "I have come to stay."

She stood up quickly. "You - WHAT? You're not staying here!"

He pushed her back on the sofa. "Oh, but I am, dear sister. Your loving husband invited me to stay while he was gone, to watch over you and keep you company." He sneered.

"He didn't! How could he? Why?" This couldn't be happening! She just couldn't be under the same roof as him with no one here to protect her!

"He was concerned about you. And he thought you would enjoy having me here to help his last week go faster. He asked me to come; how could I refuse to help my little sister?"

He reached into his bag, brought out a can, popped it open, turned the television onto a different station and sat down in a chair by the fireplace, tipping the can and drinking deeply. Marjorie shrank down in her seat and sat there, trembling with fear.

****

When the boys came in an hour later, there was a tea of bread and cheese on the kitchen table for them. They were delighted that Uncle Dickie was going to stay with them. They had enjoyed playing football with their dad and uncle. Dickie was good fun; besides playing football he said he would take them fishing and do other stuff with them.

The week progressed without incident. Marjorie could never quite relax, knowing he was in the house and she always locked her bedroom door at night. But, nothing had happened. He spent a lot of the daytimes when the boys were at school either visiting with his parents or out with friends, to Marjorie's relief. The boys enjoyed having him around; he played boisterous games with them.

He seemed to get on particularly well with John; Davey was very reserved and only joined in things when encouraged by John. Dickie and John often went out together playing when Davey stayed in to do homework. Dickie also took John on a fishing trip one morning very early, under strict orders to be home in time for John to go to school. John returned home, full of excited accounts of the trip and was hoping that Uncle Dickie would take him again some time. Dickie laughed and said of course he would. Marjorie thought that perhaps he had turned out not bad after all and began to relax a little, because they had almost got through the week with nothing nasty happening. In fact, it had been nice for the boys to have Dickie here; she admitted he had been fun, playing with them both outside and in the house. And they only had two nights and a day to get through before Tony would be home.

****

Friday afternoon came and Marjorie went out to do some shopping. They would need some things for over the weekend; they were planning to leave for their holiday on Saturday afternoon and they would need food for pack up for the journey and some to take with them because the shops would be closed on Sunday. They were booked into a holiday chalet in Rhyl, North Wales. It would only take about three hours to get there but she knew that they would probably get there too late to shop when they arrived. In order to leave Saturday morning to finish the packing and allow Tony to rest for a while before another long drive, she wanted to do as much as possible today.

When she arrived home, she was surprised that Dickie was already there and together he and John were doing toast by the kitchen range, the door of which was open. Dickie looked up as she arrived back laden with her shopping. There was a strange expression on his face, which she couldn't quite understand.

"Hello mum! Uncle Dickie and I were just doing some toast," explained John unnecessarily.

"I can see that dear." Marjorie put her bags on the table and began putting the goodies away in various cupboards. As she was doing this, Davey came in through the back door. His trousers had a hole in the knee and he was very muddy.

"Davey! What have you been doing? Look at you!" Marjorie went over to him and gave him the usual whop over the head, which he had been expecting and yet he still reeled.

"Sorry, I got pushed over," he muttered.

"Your dad is not made of money you know! You will have to make do with those trousers for a while yet. Take those things off there, don't you go a step further into the house, you dirty little baggage!"

Davey took his shoes off and made to go through.

"No! I said take them all off! I'm not having all that mud over the house! We are going away tomorrow and I've cleaned everywhere."

Davey slowly took off his trousers, letting them slip to the floor and took his socks off one by one as he lifted his feet out of his trousers. Marjorie realised for the first time just how thin he had become and suddenly she felt a pang of guilt. She watched, as did the others, as Davey almost tip-toed through the kitchen and up to his room.

"Have a bath!" Marjorie surprised herself and him. She had never told him to do that before. Usually he had to wash himself in cold water. As he sunk himself into the lovely warm water, he looked down at his own thin little body and saw the bruises of various shades on his arms, his legs and on his thighs as far as he could see, the results of the various beatings he had endured. Usually he didn't allow himself to look too closely; it only made him hate her more. The warmth of the water eased the pain in his punished body and he lingered as long as he dared. He expected her to demand that he got out, but she didn't. Obviously having Uncle Dickie here was making her happy; although he could have sworn that ever since uncle had come, she seemed even more stiff and on edge.

Dickie started drinking the minute tea was over; in fact he poured a large dose of something in his tea out of a flask from his pocket. Davey went off to do his homework, wanting to get it done before they went on holiday. Marjorie and John were downstairs with Dickie. John went into the sitting room to watch television. Marjorie was busy about the kitchen, tidying up and washing the crocks. As she dried her hands, she looked at him, sitting at the table, drinking something from a bottle.

"You've had a lot to drink already Dickie. Don't you think you've had enough?"

"A man has to have some pleasures. There aren't too many around this stinking hole."

"Well, you won't find any sitting there. Why don't you go down the pub?" she asked, hopefully hoping to get rid of him. He got up and came over to her; she mentally chastised herself: 'don't wind him up'...

He put his hand in her hair, twisted it around in his hand, and then tightened his grip so she had to look at him.

"Oh, you would like that wouldn't you sis? You want me out of here don't you? Afraid of what I might do are you?" He looked into her face; she could smell the liquor on his breath. His other hand gripped her left breast and squeezed until she squeaked in protest, even though she was desperately trying not to react. Her heart was thumping. Surely he wouldn't do anything? Not with John sitting in the other room within earshot if she screamed? She held her breath, the fear showing plainly in her face. He gave her breast a vicious pinch and released her hair so suddenly she almost fell over. She held onto the sink for support.

"Oh no sis - you don't need to worry. You are much too old for me. I have a taste for much tenderer young things than you; you should know after all! You helped me to develop my likes and needs – but now, you hold no enticements for me." As he spoke, momentarily his eyes slid towards the sitting room where John was watching television. He hastily brought his eyes back to her but not before she had seen the look and a new realisation dawned within her – and a new fear – John! If her heart had thumped before, it now felt like it would leap right out of her chest. As she looked at him, horrified, he sloped back to his chair, put his feet on the table cowboy style and resumed his drinking.

Marjorie hastened past him and went into the sitting room, saying loudly: "John! I think you should go to bed now. I know it's early but we have a long day ahead of us tomorrow. Tell Davey to go to bed too when you get up there."

"Oh, ok mum,"

"I will be up in a few minutes to say goodnight."

John went off and Marjorie busied herself in the sitting room, putting magazines and cushions tidy. Then she went upstairs. She went into John's room. He was not in bed yet but had used the bathroom.

"Can I read for a while mum?"

"Of course you can." She lowered her voice to a whisper. "And when I have gone out, lock your door behind me." She put her finger to her lips and she saw the question in his face. "Shh - don't say anything, just do as I say. Uncle Dickie is drinking a lot tonight and he can get very nasty when he is drunk, so to make sure, lock your door. I shall be locking mine too."

"Oh, ok mum."

"And if you have to visit the bathroom in the night, lock it again when you get back. Sometimes he sits up really late drinking."

"Ok. Goodnight mum. I can't wait to go on holiday tomorrow."

"Me too darling; goodnight love."

Marjorie went back downstairs. Dickie was now sitting in front of the television, still drinking steadily. Marjorie decided that she would go up to her room too, although it was much too early to go to bed. But she had packing to do and she could always read. She walked towards the kitchen door to go upstairs, then, hardly realising what she was doing, she went back, picked up the poker from beside the range then went up to her room and locked the door.

* * * * * * * * * * *

Dickie had been drinking steadily for some time. All the time he had sat there alone his mind kept going back to John. He thought about the times he had been alone with John and the things they had done and talked about. After tomorrow he was not likely to see him again, not as a child anyway. Dickie never stayed in one place long because of his 'appetites'. Oh, he had women but they were more of a cover-up for what he really liked. He often took up with young women who were alone with small children. He thought about some of the tasty little morsels he'd had recently and all of them too young to say anything...

But Dickie loved variety and now he found that his taste was lingering on the young boy upstairs. He had been grooming him this week, being his friend, gaining his confidence. He thought of John's well-fed body, imagined what it would be like to touch his naked skin; it would be so smooth, silky as only young skin can be. John was older than the ones he usually went for but there was something very childlike about him; he was young for his age - and tonight was his only chance. He had been upstairs a few times to check the light under Marjorie's door. He wanted to be sure she was asleep. It was very late, about 1.30 in the morning. She would be asleep by now for sure.

He went upstairs quietly and went to John's room. He was more than ready; he wasn't going to stop now. He turned the doorknob quietly and pushed. It never moved. He tried again. Damn! It was locked; now what was he to do? He had missed his quarry! The pain in his loins nagged at him as he stood outside the boy's door. He thought of the other boy – he was not desirable as John; he was older and so thin and scrawny. But he was small for his age too and probably not very strong; now Dickie was desperate and determined. He went to Davey's door and tried it. It opened at once. Dickie smiled to himself and started to loosen his belt.

Chapter 21

Terror

Marjorie awoke very suddenly and lay there, heart thumping, not knowing why she was awake. She lay and listened intently. Was that a noise in Davey's room? Not like him; perhaps he was going to the toilet. She listened for the soft footfall past her door but there was none. She did, however, hear what sounded like scuffling in Davey's room – what was he doing?

$$*****$$

Davey realised someone was getting into his bed but he assumed it was John, who did that sometimes when he couldn't sleep. He moved closer to the wall and resigned himself to being kept awake by John's chatter. Moments later, he realised it was someone much bigger than John. He started to get up.

"What the....?" He jumped when a large hand was clapped over his mouth.

"Shut up! Don't make a sound or it will be worse for you. Keep still."

Davey immediately stopped moving and lay, his eyes staring blindly in the dark. He knew he was facing the wall with the man behind him. He felt his pyjama trousers being roughly pulled down to his knees; he wondered what was happening. The next moment he felt searing pain. In spite of the hand over his mouth, he let out a muffled yell and at the same time in automatic reaction he brought up his right heel, which connected sharply with the soft part of the man's anatomy. The man let go of his grasp around Davey's body to writhe in pain and hold his private parts. On release of his arm Davey elbowed him as hard as he could in his chest.

Dickie wasn't used to his victims fighting back and the surprise and the dual pain rendered him useless for a moment. It was long enough for Davey to get away. He scrambled over the man, hampered at first by his pyjama bottoms still round his legs. He hastily shoved them right off; it was easier than trying to pull them up. Once he was stood on the floor, he made towards the door, only to trip and fall over something on the floor – Dickie's trousers. He made to scramble up and then screamed as a leather belt whipped down and cut into his bared back. Dickie had grabbed his belt from the bedside table and lashed out blindly in the dark after hearing Davey fall. He knew he had reached his mark and raised the belt to bring it down on the boy again.

At the sound of the scream, Marjorie shot out of bed – Davey! In her concern for John, she had forgotten to tell Davey to lock his door. But she hadn't really thought Davey was in danger. How wrong she was! She put on her dressing gown and took hold of the poker standing by her bed and padded her way quietly to Davey's room. John was just before her, in the process of opening the door. She pushed in front of him "Go away John!" she hissed at him and slammed open the door, snapping on the light.

When the door crashed open, the pair were momentarily blinded by the light flooding on.

"No!" screamed Marjorie.

Dickie laughed harshly. "And what do you care? I've heard all about how you beat this boy – I can do it properly – look!" He brought the belt down on Davey's behind and Davey screamed again.

Marjorie lunged at her brother with the poker raised. She caught him on the shoulder but didn't make much impact on him. He punched her in the face and she fell to the ground, senseless.

"Mum!" Dickie looked into the shocked eyes of John, standing terrified in the doorway.

"John!" Dickie looked towards him.

John shouted: "You have hurt my mum and my brother – I hate you! I thought you were nice but you're not!" John was talking to Dickie, but watching Davey, who was crawling towards the poker. Davey indicated – "Keep talking."

"You did all that stuff, making me like you and now you do this – and why are you undressed?"

He saw Davey pick up the poker, climb onto the bed and stand up to give him extra height. Davey slammed the poker down on Dickie's head with all the strength he could muster. It seemed the man fell in slow motion, cracking his head on the corner of the chest of drawers on his way down. He landed, half sitting, half laying in a crumpled heap on the floor, blood pouring from his head in two places. John looked at the half naked man and then retched, emptying his stomach onto the floor, tears rolling down his cheeks. He crawled towards the motionless figure of Marjorie lying on the floor, her face bloodied where the blow had cut her lip and her hair all over her face.

He looked at Davey, realising for the first time that he was half naked too.

"Davey! Why are you like that? Why is he? What's been going on?   And, oh Davey – you're hurt! Look at your back!"

Davey looked at himself as best he could; he did indeed look a mess.

"Never mind about me John - we must get help for mum. And I must get away!"

"Get away? Why must you get away?" asked John, terrified.

"I think I've killed him John! They will put me in prison; I have to get away."

There was a knocking at the door. They looked at each other, frightened. They heard a voice shouting through the letter box

"Hello, hello! We heard screaming – is everything all right in there? It's Tom from next door."

Davey was hastily pulling on some pants and some jogger bottoms, socks and a jumper. He winced as the clothes came into contact with his sore body, but he ignored it.

"You must let them in, John – but just give me time to go out of the back way. Don't tell them I'm gone; if they ask, tell them I'm staying with some friends. You must let them in so they can help mum. Tell them you don't know what happened. Go on now. I will go out the back and you lock it after me."

"I'm frightened, Davey! Can't you stay with me?"

"No! I have to get away; they will lock me up. Don't tell them anything, John. Promise me?"

"I promise Davey. Where will you go?"

"I don't know John. But I will be all right. And you will be all fine. Dad will be home tomorrow."

Davey put the landing light on and the two of them went down the stairs. The knocking continued. Davey went out into the night, his coat wrapped around him; it was pretty cold, it was the beginning of October, after all. John struggled to open the front door and let Tom in. John was crying, he didn't have to act. He pointed upstairs. Tom looked at him and ran up the stairs. He was horrified at the sight that met his eyes; the half-naked man slumped unconscious by the drawers, the woman, also unconscious crumpled on the floor.

"Good grief! What on earth has been going on here?" he asked John. John was much too upset to answer, he just kept crying. Tom checked Marjorie's pulse and then Dickie's. They were both still alive. He took hold of John's hand, took him to his bedroom and said:

"Stay there, John. I have to go next door to fetch Ann and phone for an ambulance. Do you understand?"

John nodded. Tom went off, running down the stairs and back to his own house.

"Annie love, can you go next door and look after John? I have to phone for an ambulance and the police"

"The police? Whatever has been going on?" Annie put her coat on over her nightdress and put her shoes on.

"I don't know, but it looks very suspicious to me. Don't go upstairs love, call John to come down."

Ann went next door and stood at the bottom of the stairs and called John. He came down to her slowly. She took one look at his tear-stained face and put her arms around him. He promptly burst into tears again. She led him into the sitting room where she put the gas fire on and wrapped him up in a blanket. She talked to him softly until he calmed down.

The ambulance and the police arrived almost at the same time, bells ringing, lights flashing. The police watched the doctor checking Marjorie over and examining Dickie. The police wondered what had happened – wasn't these two brother and sister? Surely there was no funny business going on between them?

Marjorie and Dickie were taken away in two ambulances. The police checked the doors and windows. There was no sign of a break in, even though it looked as though an intruder had disturbed and attacked the two adults. That didn't explain why Dickie's trousers were on the floor; very odd. The two policemen came to talk with John.

"Now young man, can you tell us what happened?" John shook his head.

"Who is the man?"

"He is my uncle," whispered John.

"And that is your stepmother I believe?"

"Yes"

"Why was your uncle here?"

"He has been staying with us this week."

"I see. Where is your father?"

"Dad works away. He will be home in the morning. We were going on holiday tomorrow."

"I see. Where does your dad work?"

"I don't know."

"Do you know why your mother and your uncle were in the same bedroom?"

"No. It is my brother Davey's bedroom."

"Is that so? And where is your brother?"

"I don't know."

"Is my mother going to die?" John burst into tears again.

"No son, your mum will be fine. They will make her better in the hospital."

John cried and cried and would not be soothed. Ann said she didn't think they should bother John any more than night. The police agreed. Ann said they would look after John for the rest of the night; she didn't think they should take him anywhere, especially as his father would be home the next day.

Out in the hallway, the policeman had a quiet word with Tom.

"Perhaps you would keep an eye out for Mr. Adams and give us a call when he gets home, sir. We will need to talk with him."

"Of course. What about the other boy, Davey? He doesn't seem to be here."

"The younger boy just said he doesn't know where he is," replied the policeman.

"Hmm, that's funny," said Tom.

"What's the other boy like?"

"Well, he is twelve but he is very small for his age; he looks half-starved and he is very quiet. Ann and I often wonder if they treat him right."

"Oh yes, I remember now; we picked him up for shoplifting once. I remember thinking he looked starved then. But the mother told us all about how they had been abandoned and she was trying to get them sorted."

"That was years ago! The boys were only five and six! They were in Beaumont House for a few years. And they have been living here for about eighteen months or more now; that should be plenty of time to make things right."

"Hmm," the policeman was thoughtful. Could this be a case of child abuse? There was certainly something very strange going on here. Perhaps he would contact Social Services and see if they know anything. But it was weekend now, so that would have to wait until Monday. He looked at his watch, it showed three – ten. Perhaps he could get a cuppa back at the station.

****

Davey had listened while John let in the neighbour and once Tom was in and upstairs, Davey quietly slipped away through the back garden and into the neighbours' garden. He managed to get over the fence to the next garden and the next. Then he made his way to the front of the houses and crouched down as a police car and two ambulances raced up the road to his house.

Once they were all in the house, he made his way down the road, keeping near the hedges. It was painful to walk because his bottom hurt, as did his back where the strap had cut him. He also had a pain in his chest and he was struggling to breathe. His progress was slow as he made his way towards the main road. He knew he had to go towards the city; he had to go over the river. He had never been this far in this direction on his own before. In the dark he wasn't all that sure where he was going. His steps were getting harder, he was going slower. He didn't really know where he was going; his only thought was he had to find Aunty Sally. He knew if he could find her, she would make everything come right....

Chapter 22

A Place of Safety

At the time the policeman was looking at his watch at 3.10 a.m., Davey was crossing the river over the Old Bridge. He had chosen to go that way in case any police cars went over the New Bridge. He didn't like being out in the dark over much; the Old Bridge was a bit spooky at night. But he was very nervous of being discovered so it was easier to keep to shadows this way. He slipped round the corner and saw the Cathedral in front of him. He knew roughly where he was. Keeping a sharp look out for policemen, he continued walking down Broad Street. There was absolutely no one about, for which Davey was grateful. But he was cold now, and it was beginning to rain. As he turned the corner and looked towards High Town, he thought about Beaumont House; he thought he could find it from here, it was the other side of the town and up the hill. He thought of Emily matron; perhaps she could help him find Aunty Sally.

He moved through High Town like a little shadow, keeping near the buildings and fading into doorways if he saw anyone. He eventually came to where he had to cross Blue School Street and continue up the road past the bus station. He recognised the area and knew he was going the right way. It was hard going; he was wet as well as cold now. He was glad he had his duffel coat on; it was keeping the worst of the wet out, but it wasn't a waterproof coat.

As he went over the railway bridge, he suddenly realised where he was and had another thought – Joe! Joe lived near here and it would be much easier than going up the hill; Davey was so very tired now. And the hill was very scary in the dark; also Davey was worried that Emily matron might call the police. Joe would know where Sally was wouldn't he? After all, she was his girlfriend.....Davey's mind was becoming befuddled; he had entirely forgotten that she had married someone else. He turned to the left just past the railway station and went along Barrs Court Road, his feet dragging; he could hardly walk. He was feeling ill, his head ached, his body hurt, he hardly knew what he was doing. Only the thought of finding Sally was driving him on now.

He finally came to Joe's house. He had no idea what time it was. There were two bottles of milk on the doorstep already. Davey, exhausted, slumped down on the step, heedless of sitting in the wet and huddled down in his coat and in spite of the rain and cold, fell asleep.

****

Joe could never sleep in on a Saturday; he was so used to being up early for work. He came downstairs wearing his pyjamas and put the kettle on for a cup of tea. He made a pot of tea because he knew his mum would be down very shortly. He went to the fridge to get the milk. He took out the bottle and there was only a drop left. So he went to get the milk from the front doorstep. The milkman always came really early, between 4.30 and 5a.m. so he knew it would be there as it was now just after 7.30a.m.

He opened the door and bent down to pick up the bottles, when he saw what appeared to be a bundle of clothes on the doorstep.

"What on earth....?"

He stepped outside, even though it was wet and he was wearing slippers, to investigate. He pulled the hood of the coat back to find it revealed the face and head of a boy. He looked closer...

"My goodness - I think it's Davey!"

He shook the figure a bit and Davey's eyes flickered open slightly. "Aunty Sally?"

The voice was so quiet that Joe hardly heard him. As he looked into the boy's face, realised that the lad was sick, very sick. He gathered him up in his arms – he was much lighter than Joe had expected.

He carried Davey into the house, calling for his mum. He took Davey into the kitchen as it was the warmest room at that time because the gas burner was on. He sat and held him like a baby. He looked up as his mother hastened into the room in answer to his call. She stopped short when she saw Joe sitting on a kitchen chair cradling what was clearly a boy in very wet clothes.

"Goodness, Joe! What's that? Who is it? How is he here?"

"Mum, its Davey – you remember - from Beaumont House? He used to come here with Sally."

"Yes, I remember Davey! What is he doing here?"

"I don't know. I just found him asleep on our doorstep. I think he's very sick, mum."

"I will put the fire on in the sitting room. We must get his wet things off and get him dry and warm."

Gladys hastened out of the room, lit the gas fire in the sitting room then went upstairs to get towels and blankets. When she came down, Joe carried Davey into the sitting room and sat down with him still on his lap on the sofa in front of the fire. He began to remove the boy's clothes. Davey let him take off his coat without protest, but when Gladys moved forward to remove his wet trousers, he would not let her. She misunderstood what he meant and said gently:

"It's all right, Davey lad, I understand you are too big to be undressed by a woman. I will go away so that Joe can do it. You are very wet and you will be ill if we don't get you dry."

Davey didn't want Joe to undress him either but eventually gave in and let him do it; he was so ill he just had no strength to resist further. As Joe peeled the boy's clothes off him, he was shocked at how thin he was and even more so when he saw so many bruises of various colours all over the lad's arms and legs. And when he took Davey's top clothes off and saw the red wheals on his back and the spots of blood on his t-shirt, he was even more appalled – grief! What had been going on? Who had done this to this boy?

"Mum! Come and look at this!"

Gladys came in and Joe lifted the big bath towel which he had wrapped around Davey to show her the lad's back. She was shocked. Mother and son looked at each other in anguish.

"Poor little fellow!" Gladys had tears running down her cheeks. "Who would do such a thing? And he looks half-starved too! No wonder he has run away!"

"We should call the police," Joe looked at his mum. Davey struggled up:

"No! Please! Don't tell the police; they will take me away. I want Aunty Sally, please Joe, I need Aunty Sally."

"There, there Davey lad, don't get upset. We won't call the police. No one is going to take you away. You are safe here."

Gladys and Joe wrapped Davey up in some blankets and laid him down on the sofa.

"Now Davey, don't you worry about anything. Auntie Gladys will look after you while you have a nice sleep. When you wake up, Aunty Sally will be here. I'm going to get her for you. Sleep now."

Joe watched as Davey once more slipped into sleep and then he went upstairs to get dressed. He went back downstairs to drink a mug of tea that his mum had poured out for him and eat some toast she had made. It was still quite early; it was about 8.30 by then and he was worried that, not only was it early to call on Sally, but also worried that she would not listen to him. He voiced these worries to his mum.

"You have to try, son! Obviously, whatever has gone on with Davey, he has run away to try to find Sally.

She is who he needs and wants right now. She will know what to do once she has seen him."

"You're right, mum. I will go now and see what I can do." Joe went to fetch a jacket and his car keys. "I will be back as soon as I can."

As Joe started up his car and headed off towards the Roman Road, he suddenly felt he should enlist the help of Sally's mum, so headed the car in the direction of Manvers.

****

Sally was surprised to hear a knock at the door so early on a Saturday morning; she had just had breakfast with Jess and was with her in the sitting room. She was even more surprised to see her mother upon opening the door.

"Hello Mum! This is a surprise – come in," Sally opened the door wider so her mum could step inside.

"Gan'ma!" Jess toddled towards Maureen, who scooped her up and gave her a kiss. Still holding Jess, she turned to Sally.

"I am here with Joe, Sally,"

"Joe?" Sally's heart leaped. "But why? What's going on?"

"He has some serious news for you, love, about Davey. Will you let him in?"

"Davey? Yes, yes of course, let him in." Sally watched as her mother went back to the door and signalled to Joe, who was sitting in the car, waiting anxiously. He immediately got out and came to the house.

"Hello, Sally."

"Hello, Joe. What's this about Davey? Has something happened to him? And how do you know about it?"

They sat down in the sitting room and Joe explained as quickly as he could the happenings of the morning. Sally listened and a tear rolled down her cheek. Joe felt his heart twist at the sight of it. Sally stood up.

"I must go to him at once! Will you look after Jess for me, mum?"

"Of course – that's why I've come. I knew you would go to Davey. Your dad will come here when he's finished work at twelve. Don't worry about Jess; be as long as you need to be."

"Thank you mum," Sally kissed her mum and Jess on their cheeks and grabbed her coat from the peg in the hallway and, when indicated by Joe, preceded him out of the door. Maureen stood with Jess in her arms waving from the doorway. She watched the car drive away and then closed the door and went inside.

Sally and Joe said very little on the ride to Joe's house, although they were each very aware of the other.

"What's been going on with him, Joe?" she asked eventually.

"I can't begin to imagine, Sal. One thing is for sure, that boy has been through some terrible things."

"I was so worried when his father married Marjorie. But I had no idea it would come to something like this."

"I didn't know he had married Marjorie," Joe frowned. "How on earth did that happen I wonder?"

"No. No, of course you wouldn't. It happened after we, after I, married Evan. I think, from what I was told that Marjorie saw Mr. Adams one day and then went all out to get him."

"That sounds like Marjorie," he said grimly. "They should never have let Davey go home."

"Well, from what I know, Emily matron tried to warn the child care officer but there was little she could actually do to stop it."

They were soon at Joe's house and Sally followed Joe indoors. She smiled shyly at Gladys, who said "hello, Sally; I'm glad you have come. Davey is in here."

Sally looked at the sleeping boy, then knelt down beside him on the floor and felt for his hand. At her touch, the boy stirred and opened his eyes. He looked at her sleepily. She smiled at him.

"Hello, Davey love."

"Aunty Sally. I knew you would come. I need you, Aunty Sally." His voice was weak.

"And here I am. You know I am always here for you. Everything is all right, sweetheart." She smoothed her hand around his face, stroking back his hair. He smiled, and drifted off to sleep again.... he knew things would be ok now...

Sally sat with him for a while; then she said to Joe and Gladys:

"He is very sick; I think he should be in hospital. And the police should be told; they are probably looking for him." They were nodding in agreement when Davey cried a weak cry: "No! No, please, don't take me to hospital! Don't tell the police! They will take me away, they will lock me up!"

"There now, my darling, don't you fret, we won't tell the police or send you to hospital," soothed Sally, looking at the others with a worried frown. What could they do?

"Joe, will you take me and Davey back to my house please? I will look after him there and get the doctor to look at him. We have to get him well, and then we will think about what to do next."

Joe nodded. Sally spoke quietly to Davey in his ear: "Davey love, we are going to take you to my house so I can look after you. Is that ok?"

Davey nodded, ever so slightly. Joe gathered him up, blankets and all, and carried him out to the car. Sally got in the back seat so she could hold Davey's head on her lap. Joe drove as smoothly as he could back to Sally's house, where he carried Davey in and laid him on the sofa.

Sally went upstairs to make the bed in the spare bedroom and put a hot water bottle in to warm it. Joe helped Davey to visit the bathroom, and then popped him into the bed. Sally encouraged Davey to take a little drink and then he lay down to sleep again. She left him to sleep and went downstairs.

"He needs a doctor, but I don't have a phone."

"There is a phone box just down the road," said Maureen. "I will go and phone from there."

"Oh, thank you, mum."

Joe had gone into the kitchen to make Sally a cup of tea. She drank it thankfully. Jess was happily playing with her toys in the room. As they sat there, drinking in companionable silence, Jess came up to Joe, bringing a toy for him to see. She held it out to him and he took it, looking at it carefully, then she put her arms up for him to lift her. He brought her onto his knee and cuddled her, remembering how he used to play with her before, a few months ago. Did she remember him? She did seem to.

Sally watched as Joe played with Jess and they looked so happy together; what a fool she had been! Now he was someone else's husband. It wasn't long before her mother arrived back home after phoning the doctor.

"He said he would be here very shortly," she reported. Sally made her mum a coffee and then went back upstairs to check on Davey. He was still sleeping, but he was so hot now. She drew back the covers and unwrapped the blankets belonging to Gladys from around the hot little body. When she saw how dreadfully thin he was, the blood on his back from where the belt had struck him and all the bruises, she gasped. Poor Davey; he looked like he had been almost starved and had been hit a lot over a long period of time. She was so upset and angry. She covered him with just the sheet in order to cool him a bit; she would normally have sponged him down but she didn't want to destroy any 'evidence', because the doctor had to see all this...

It was indeed a very short time before the doctor arrived. This was a doctor from the surgery she attended and she knew him quite well. She stayed in the room while the doctor examined him very carefully, having been given a run-down of events by Joe and Maureen before he came upstairs. Davey was hardly aware of what was happening as his fever raged. The doctor covered him up again and indicated to Sally that she should come out of the room with him. They went downstairs into the sitting room, where Joe, Maureen and Jim, who had just arrived, sat waiting. The doctor looked very serious indeed.

"The boy is, indeed very sick; he should go to hospital."

Sally protested at this, explaining that Davey was afraid of going to hospital and she had promised she wouldn't let him go there.

"If you tell me what to do, I will look after him here," she said. "I will watch over him day and night until he is well again."

"We will help," said Maureen.

"Very well, I will leave him here. But there is something else I must tell you. Besides being systematically starved over a prolonged period of time and beaten and whipped, he has also been sexually abused, very recently."

There was a shocked silence. For a few moments there was no sound except for Jess's movements with her toys.

"But, but how could that happen?" blurted Sally. "Marjorie could starve him and beat him, but I'm sure she couldn't do something like that. And I don't believe his father would do it either. And Davey has said something about being afraid they will lock him up; all very strange."

"At a guess, I would say that this new assault has something to do with why he ran away. I'm sorry, but I have to inform the police about this."

"You are right doctor," Jim had said little until now. "The police must be brought in to this. Even without the - the last bit, they should have to be told because he has run away and they will be looking for him."

"I can't help wondering about John," worried Sally. "Do you think he is all right?"

She wasn't asking anyone in particular, wasn't expecting an answer really. The doctor gathered his things.

"I must go. I will contact the police for you. Don't wash him; they will need to take photographic evidence. Horrible I know, but it will need to be done. Here is a prescription which you can get filled at the duty chemist in Widemarsh Street. Give it every four hours, and plenty of liquids if you can. After the police have been, you can sponge him down when he is hot and keep him warm when he is cold; you know how to do it Sally."

"Yes I do; thank you doctor." She saw him out.

Maureen said that she and Jim should take Jess and go and do the shopping. She felt Jess should be out of the way when the police came in case it frightened her. She also felt that Sally needed to concentrate on Davey right now. Sally agreed. Joe said he would go get the prescription filled.

After they had all gone, Sally went upstairs to watch over Davey. She prayed that he would get well soon and that everything would be sorted out. She also prayed that she would be able to keep him so she could make sure he was never hurt again...

Joe was soon back with the medication, which was in liquid form to make it easy for Davey to take. She immediately gave him a dose. Just as she had done that, the police arrived.

Before they went upstairs, Joe and Sally told the police everything that had happened. The policeman noted it all down solemnly. He had with him a photographer, who was going to take pictures of the evidence. They went upstairs and Sally gently soothed Davey and told him not to worry; they just needed to look at his back again. Davey trusted her and turned obediently so the photographer could take the pictures. Davey was hardly aware of anything anyway. The police officer realised that the boy would not be able to talk with him, he was much too ill, so he went back downstairs to talk with Sally again.

"There was an incident during the night when we were called in to a house over the river. I'm wondering if this boy is connected to that incident. I will have to go back to the station to read the reports about it. I believe there was a boy who couldn't be accounted for. There are more investigations going on today."

"Well, I do know they lived over the other side of the river," said Sally. "Davey has a younger brother called John. I'm worried about him."

The policeman snapped his book shut. "I will see what I can find out. We will be in touch again. Hopefully we will be able to talk with Davey in a few days when he is better."

After she had shown the police out, she turned to Joe.

"Thank you for all you have done, Joe," she said. "But you had better not stay any longer; you'd better get home. I can manage now."

"I'm staying."

"But you have been here for ages! Your wife will wonder what is going on."

There was a silence for a moment, the Joe said quietly:

"I have no wife, Sally."

"But you got married in September! The first Saturday, you said."

"I did say, but I didn't get married, Sally."

"You didn't? Why not?" Sally's heart seemed to stand still.

"I broke it off with her soon after you and I quarrelled. I knew I didn't love her enough to marry her."

"You didn't love her?"

"No. I didn't realise until I met you again. I realised that I was going along with the marriage because I couldn't have you, you were married to Evan. Then, after we quarrelled, I knew I couldn't marry her; it would be wrong to marry anyone when I love you, have always loved you, ever since you gave me a chip."

Sally looked at him; there were tears in her eyes again.

"I heard church bells on the day you were to be married and I thought I had lost you for ever. I'm so sorry, Joe; I'm so stupid. I think being married to Evan messed up my head. He made me think that all men only wanted sex. I thought you were the same. I should have known better."

"Well, perhaps you should have, but I didn't handle things very well did I? So we are both to blame. But I love you, Sally; I don't want anyone else. Will you be my girl again, please?"

By way of answer, Sally went into his arms and they held each other tight. They didn't know what terrible things had happened to Davey, or how it would resolve, but they had him to thank for bringing them together again.

Chapter 23

A Shock for Tony

When Tony Adams arrived home soon after 9.30 a.m., he opened the front door and called for his family. He was puzzled that the house was so quiet; it had a deserted feel about it. He walked through the downstairs, looking in all the rooms. The kitchen had no sign of breakfast having been had, no fresh washing up drying on the draining board. He went upstairs and looked in his bedroom; the room was empty, the covers of the bed turned back as though Marj had just climbed out of bed.

He went next into Davey's room and that too was empty, although he almost walked into some sick on the floor. As he walked in he saw a pair of men's trousers on the floor near the bed – how odd! And then he noticed blood on the chest of drawers and on the floor near the drawers – good grief! What has happened here? An accident? Panic started to rise in Tony throat – and then there was a knock at the door. He raced downstairs and wrenched the door open. There stood his neighbour, Tom.

"Tom! Oh!" Tony didn't know what to say.

"Tony, I'm glad you are home. I have John at our house, will you come over?"

"You have John? Why do you have John? Where are Marjorie, Dickie, and Davey?"

"Come on mate, come and have a cup of tea and I will tell you what's gone on."

Tony followed Tom next door, his heart churning, his mind full of questions. He took the cup of tea offered and sat at the table in the kitchen.

"Tony, something happened at your house last night. We heard screaming...."

"Screaming?" Tony head shot up.

"Yes, and I went round to see if Marjorie needed any help. John let me in and I found Marjorie and Dickie unconscious in Davey's bedroom. Davey wasn't there."

"What? Where is Marjorie, where is my wife?"

"They took her to hospital and Dickie too."

Tony got up. "I must go and see her!"

Tom got up too. "You can't go yet Tony; the police want to see you. I'm supposed to let them know when you are home."

"Well, they will have to see me at the hospital then! I must see Marjorie."

"Don't you want to see John?"

"Oh, John – yes of course, where is he?"

At that moment, John came into the kitchen, still dressed in his pyjamas. On seeing his father, he rushed to him.

"Dad! Oh Dad!" and he burst into tears. Tony sat down again and pulled his son to sit beside him. He put his arm around him.

"John has refused to tell us anything about what happened, Tony," said Ann as she came into the room. "He wouldn't talk to the police."

Tony said gently to his son, "John, do you know what happened?" John nodded his head.

"Will you tell me about it?"

"Davey said not to tell," said John.

"Where is Davey?" asked Tony.

"I don't know," sobbed John. "He ran away. Oh daddy, I am frightened."

"Why did Davey run away?" Tony asked. John stared at him unhappily; what should he do? Should he tell dad even though Davey said not to?

"It's beginning to look like Davey went mad and hurt his mother and his uncle somehow," began Tom, "Although how a small lad like him could do that I don't know."

"No!" John burst out. "It wasn't Davey's fault. It was Uncle Dickie's. He is a bad man daddy! But Davey was afraid that he killed Uncle Dickie so he ran away."

Tony looked at his son in horror – what on earth had happened?

"Come on, John, tell me what happened," he coaxed gently. "It's fine to tell your dad."

So John told Tony what he had seen. Tony was puzzled what Dickie had been doing in Davey's room in the first place.

"Mum said that Uncle Dickie had been drinking a lot and he gets nasty when he's drunk a lot. She told me to lock my door when I went to bed but she must have forgotten to tell Davey and he got in there. Mum tried to save Davey but Uncle Dickie knocked her down. Then Davey hit Uncle Dickie with the poker and he fell and hit his head on the drawers. He was bleeding a lot and Davey thought he had killed him. He was very frightened and he ran away."

Tony hugged his son and told him he was a good boy for telling him what had happened.

"I am going see your mum, John. Do you want to come with me, or do you want to stay here with Tom and Ann?"

"Can I come, dad? I want to see if she is all right."

"Of course. Come on, we will go next door and get you dressed and then we'll go."

He turned to Tom and Ann.

"Thank you very much for looking after John for me. Would you tell the police that I am at the hospital please?"

"Of course. I do hope Marjorie will recover quickly and that Davey will be found."

Davey! What could he do about him? Tony hardly knew what he was doing. When the police came he would have to tell them that his son was missing.

It only took a few minutes to get to the hospital in the car although parking was difficult because it was Saturday and the town was filling up quickly with shoppers. They were shown into a room where Marjorie was alone. Tony looked into the face of his wife laying so still, her once lovely face very badly bruised with a cut just under her eye. Apart from the purple part of her face, she was very pale. Tony went over and sat by her bed, taking her hand in his. John stood beside him. At the feel of his hand, Marjorie's eyes flickered open and she turned her head slightly to look at him. As she did so, tears trickled down her face.

"Tony, my love," her voice was faint and croaky. "I'm sorry, I'm so sorry."

"Shh! It's all right my darling. I'm here. I'm the one who is sorry; I wish I had come home last night and I certainly wish I hadn't asked Dickie to stay while I was gone."

"I wish you hadn't too, but you didn't know. I tried to stop him. I tried to stop him hurting Davey..."

"I know you did, my brave love. John told me everything that happened."

"But you don't understand...."

"It's all right, love. All you have to do now is get better. Don't try to talk anymore. There will be plenty of time to talk when you are better."

Marjorie closed her eyes; he was right, there would be plenty of time to talk...

John was glad to see that she was awake; she looked terrible but if she could talk she would get better.

As they sat there, the door opened and a police officer came in.

"May I speak with you sir?"

Tony got up and, followed by John, he went out of the room.

"Are you Anthony Adams of 54 Wellbeck Road, Hereford?"

"Yes. You know I am."

"I would like you to come down to the station to assist us in our enquiries. Is this your son?"

"Yes. This is my youngest son, John."

"We would like to talk with him too."

"Is it necessary for us to come to the station?" asked Tony, puzzled.

"Yes sir. This is a complicated matter and my superiors wish to see you."

Tony and John followed the officer out of the hospital and into the police car. John thought it was quite exciting to ride in a police car! Once at the police station, John was introduced to a policewoman and was told they wanted to speak with his dad first, so would he like to go with PW Smith and get something to eat? John went with the woman and Tony was taken to an interview room.

What followed was quite traumatic for Tony; it seemed they thought he had done it! They thought that he had come back in the night to find something strange going on between the brother and sister and attacked them both! Tony was thankful he could tell them where he was the evening until quite late and that he had been seen checking out of his hotel in Essex just before six that morning. It was impossible that he would have had time to drive home and back to his hotel in the time. He was with his bosses still at 1.30 a.m. and the incident at his house was happening at around that time. Yes, he had plenty of witnesses as to his whereabouts at that time.

"You need to talk with John; he knows what happened."

"We are going to see him now sir. I regret that we had to put you through that at this time but we had to be sure. In many cases of this nature it is the husband that has done it!"

John was brought in and, with encouragement from his father, told the inspector what had happened. The inspector was a big man, rather ruddy in complexion with grey hair which curled quite tightly. In spite of his size, he was quite quietly spoken and was gentle with the boy. He listened intently to John's story without interruption.

"Do you know why your uncle was in your brother's room?" he asked John once the boy had stopped talking.

"No sir. Mum had told me to lock my door because she said Uncle Dickie got nasty when he was drunk. So perhaps that was it sir."

"Yes....hmm.... and what about your brother Davey? Do you have any idea where he might have gone?"

"No sir."

"Right, ok lad. You have done very well. I think you and your dad can go now."

"Please sir, you won't lock Davey up will you? He didn't mean to kill Uncle Dickie!"

"No son, we are not going to lock Davey up. Your uncle isn't dead, although he isn't in too good a shape just now! And it rather sounds as though he deserved what he got! But we do need to find your brother."

The inspector saw them out of his office and said that the police officer who brought them would take them back to the hospital to collect Tony's car.

"We will make a search for Davey sir. We will get in touch with you if we find anything. And if he comes home, perhaps you will let us know."

"Of course; thank you." Tony was thankful to be leaving the police station and put his arm protectively round John's shoulders. The ride back to the hospital was soon over and they went to collect their car. They bought fish and chips and drove home to see if Tom and Ann had heard anything about Davey.

After they had eaten, Tony felt he should go and see Marjorie's parents, who probably had no idea what had happened. He took John with him. He just didn't know how he was going to tell Bill and Margaret about it, especially as it seemed their son was the cause of it all.

They were, indeed, very shocked at the news and Margaret wanted to go and see her daughter in the hospital. Tony agreed to take her, so they left John with Bill and went to see Marjorie. Margaret was very tearful when she saw the battered face of her daughter; she just couldn't believe her son could do that to his own sister. She decided she wanted to see Dickie and asked where he was. She was directed to a room on its own. There was a policeman outside the door and another inside the room. Although it seemed there was little need, for Dickie looked as if he was still out cold, his head bandaged. She looked at him and took his hand.

"Why did you hit your sister, my son?" she whispered but there was no answer forthcoming from him. She wasn't to know that he was actually not unconscious and could hear her but he didn't want to talk to her, so he was lying very still and hoping she would go away... She did go away and he was glad, for what could he say to her? He felt that this was probably the end of the line for him.

She went back to Marjorie's room. Tony was sitting by her side, holding her hand and talking to her. Upon seeing his mother- in- law he got up and indicated she should sit near her daughter. She sat down and stroked her daughter's hand. Marjorie opened her eyes, saw her mother and again the tears welled up.

"Mum."

"There, there my love, you will soon be better. Don't cry; although I know it must hurt a lot."

"It does mum," although Marjorie was talking about inside....she wished so much that she had told her mum about Dickie all those years ago. But she was afraid of him; also afraid her mum would not believe her. She wondered how many children had been so hurt, possibly damaged forever by her brother. Perhaps if she had spoken out, they would have been saved; and perhaps she would have been, and Davey too....

Davey! The thoughts of him made the tears trickle again. She had been so cruel to him; all because he reminded her of Dickie. Dickie looked as if butter wouldn't melt in his mouth; no one would ever have suspected what he was capable of. But Davey looked that way because he was what he appeared to be – a gentle boy who cared for his brother and did what he could to protect him. He had just needed to be loved; instead she had given him a life of pain and trauma.

A nurse came in and saw Marjorie's distress. She decided that she should have some medication to make her sleep. She told Tony and Margaret that she was going to put Marjorie to sleep for a while so they should go and rest.

Tony took Margaret home and reported to Bill and John on Marjorie's condition. A knock came at the door. It was the police officer who had driven them earlier. They asked him in.

"I have news for you sir. It seems that your son Davey is found."

"Thank goodness! Where is he, officer?"

"He is at a house over the river. It seems he went in search of an Aunty from Beaumont House who he was particularly fond of. He is at her house. But he is very sick sir."

"Sick?" Tony felt he couldn't take much more. "Can I see him?"

"Yes sir. I will take you over there."

Joe opened the door to the policeman and Davey's father. He took them upstairs. They saw a still figure in the single bed and a small, slim woman sitting beside him, watching over him. She looked very young, hardly in her late teens with her thin frame and pony tail. She stood up as they came in and watched as Tony Adams went over to his son.

"Davey," At the sound of his father's voice, Davey's eyes flickered but stayed closed. Tony could see he was very ill.

"He is ill because he was out all night in the cold and the wet and he was in a much weakened state," Sally told him quietly.

"Why isn't he in hospital?" asked Tony.

"He didn't want to go; he was afraid. And he trusts me, Mr. Adams. I couldn't break that trust. He needs to know he can trust someone."

"I appreciate everything you have done, erm, Sally, but I should take him home now."

"I can't let you do that Mr. Adams!" he was surprised that this frail looking little thing should suddenly get so fierce!

"Do you have any idea what he has gone through? They will not let him live with Marjorie again after what she has done to him."

Tony was stunned.

"What are you talking about? What has Marjorie done to him?"

"See for yourself!" Sally gently folded the covers back so he could see the thin, emaciated body and the bruises of all shades. Tony was horrified.

"Marjorie has done that? I don't believe it!"

"You had better believe it. I'm sorry to tell you this, but Marjorie treated him badly when she was his housemother at Beaumont House. Emily matron and I and everyone were very worried when you married her and had the boys home."

She felt very sorry for this poor man, who obviously loved his son and loved his wife and couldn't believe what he was hearing.

"But she let me think she loved the boys, and I thought they loved her!"

"Well, she did get on well with John and him with her, but there was something about Davey that seemed to wind her up somehow. I tried very hard to get to the bottom of it, but Marjorie would never tell me anything. Come downstairs Mr. Adams. There is something else I need to tell you but I don't want Davey hearing too much."

Once downstairs, Sally told him about the sexual abuse and the whipping. He sat down and put his head in his hands. Oh god, what a mess! He knew who had whipped Davey, having heard John's account and suddenly the pieces started to fall into place.

"My goodness, it was him - her brother! She tried to tell me she didn't want him around but I never understood; I thought she would be pleased to have company while I was away. She was afraid of him. My goodness, if I had known I wouldn't have let him anywhere near my family."

He told Sally and Joe about what had happened in the night. Sally immediately understood why Davey feared they would lock him up. He would need to be told as soon as he was well enough to understand, that he hadn't killed Dickie. It was difficult to believe that Davey had had enough strength to hit Dickie hard enough to knock him over, but she also realised that fear had given him strength, not only to do that but to keep him walking through the night in spite of his weakened state. She was also glad to know that John was safe and well.

"It sounds as if Marjorie was trying to protect Davey; that's one point in her favour," Joe had said little up to now. "I think this need to be looked into further, officer." He looked up at the policeman, who was still there with them. He nodded. "It certainly does sir."

Tony Adams stood up to go; although he didn't really know what to do now.

"Thank you for taking care of Davey. I can see he needs to remain here. He is too sick to move and anyway, I can see that I'm going to have much to do with Marjorie in hospital and John to look after."

"You can come and see Davey when you like Mr. Adams," said Sally. "You can be sure I will do my best to make him well. I have always loved him and, if you will excuse me saying so, I've always thought of him as my boy." She walked towards her display shelves and took something down. She held it up for him to see.

"Davey gave me this tiger key-ring once after he had won it at the Mayfair because he loved me and wanted to give me something. I have always kept it because he is important to me. He is a very brave little boy, and when he was damaged so badly that he couldn't cope anymore he came looking for me, knowing I would help him. And you know, Marjorie is a damaged person; who knows what that brute of a brother did to her? I have always thought there was something. I hope you can find it in your heart to forgive her and help her because she is going to need you even more now."

Tony was amazed at the understanding this slip of a girl had; she had given him much to think about. He bade them goodbye and preceded the policeman out of the door.

Chapter 24

Revelations

Davey's fever raged all Saturday night. Sally had a put-you-up bed which she made up and put in the room with him so she could be there to keep an eye on him. She sponged him down regularly throughout the night and watched over him. Joe watched over them all. He helped her get Jess ready for bed and kept her supplied with food and drinks and also brought fresh water for Davey to drink or be washed in. He slept in Sally's bedroom because she was in Davey's room. In the morning Jim and Maureen came round to bring food for dinner – 'we will cook here; it seems sensible' – and to take Jess to church with them, for she would be looked after in the crèche there, she would enjoy it and it would give Sally a break for an hour or so.

While her parents and Jess were gone to church, Joe insisted that Sally go to her bed to have a proper sleep, for he knew she had only cat-napped throughout the night. It was bliss to sink into the comfort of her own bed and Sally was soon peacefully sleeping. Joe watched over Davey, who was now sleeping peacefully too, the fever was leaving his body. Sally got up when her parents came home with Jess and went to look at Davey. She felt his forehead and it felt almost normal. At her touch, he opened his eyes.

"Aunty Sally! You really are here. I've been having such strange dreams all about running away and being with you and Granddad Jim and Granny Mo were here, and, and, Joe...."

"Well dear, they weren't dreams; they really happened. You are at my house with Granddad and Granny and Joe. You have been very poorly and we have been looking after you."

Suddenly Davey struggled to sit up. He looked very frightened.

"Do the police know I'm here?"

"Yes dear, they do. And you have no need to worry. Your uncle isn't dead, you didn't kill him, Davey. No one is going to take you away. You are going to stay here with me. Do you understand, Davey love?"

"Is it true? I didn't kill him? I'm safe then? Do I have to go back to be with Mother?"

"No Davey, I said you are going to stay here with me. You will not go back to be with her again, although your dad will want to see you, and John."

"John! Is he all right?"

"Yes, John is fine.

Your dad is home now and is looking after him."

Davey sat and thought about all that and then he said:

"Aunty Sally?"

"Yes love?"

"I'm hungry."

Sally threw her arms around him and hugged him.

"Well, is that so? We will see what we can do about that! Granny Mo is cooking dinner right now. It won't be long. Do you feel like getting up for a little while?"

Davey nodded. So Sally wrapped him up in her own dressing gown which was lovely and warm "Oh, you do look funny Davey!" And she was thrilled to see him giggle.

****

When Tony went to see Marjorie in hospital the next day, she was awake and sitting up in bed. She smiled tentatively at him as he came in.

"Hello darling," Tony kissed her on her cheek and sat down near her. "I'm so glad you see you awake again. How are you feeling now?"

"My face hurts," she said. "But I deserve it."

"No you do not! You did your best to save Davey." He was dismayed to see her burst into tears.

"But you don't understand..."

"Oh yes I think I do. Why didn't you tell me about Dickie, Marj? Why couldn't you trust me enough to tell me what he did to you?"

"You, you know?" she whispered.

"Well, put it this way, I have a fair idea. Won't you tell me about it, dear?"

Marjorie gulped; but she knew she had to now. So, for the first time ever, she told another person all about the hellish nightmare of a life she had lived with her brother, starting at the age of six for four, terrible years. As he listened, Tony's face went white; he wanted to kill Dickie with his bare hands! He didn't interrupt until she had finished telling him all the dreadful details. Once she started, it was like opening a floodgate and it all came spilling out of her in a torrent, on and on, the tears spilling down her face the whole time. When she had finished, she cried as if her heart would break, great sobs that wracked her whole body. Tony put his arms around her and just held her until the sobs gradually subsided.

"There now love, there now; I'm here and I love you. I will help you, my love."

"Oh Tony, I'm not worth it! I've done terrible things to poor Davey, all because he reminded me of Dickie. I think I was punishing him for what Dickie did to me. Davey will never want to come near me again so I can't stay with you."

"Davey has a loving heart; I think he will forgive you once he understands. And I think Dickie has played his own part in making Davey know what he does," said Tony grimly. Marjorie stared at him in horror.

"He didn't! He didn't do – that – to Davey?"

"I certainly think he might have tried. We can't ask him at the moment because Davey is very poorly; he ran away and caught a chill being out in the rain all night."

"He's ill? Poor Davey and it's my entire fault. Where is he? Who is looking after him?"

"He is with someone called Sally; she was an aunty at Beaumont House. It appears he ran away to find her."

"Sally! Yes, she always loved him and he loved her. I should never have kept him away from her. Sally is a very caring girl; she tried very hard to be my friend when we worked together. I think she knew there was something with me but I couldn't bring myself to tell her."

"When I leave you I shall go and see him again and when I come back this evening I will be able to tell you more about how he is."

"Oh Tony; do you hate me now? You must do, knowing what I did to your son." She looked at him tearfully and he could see the fear in her eyes.

"No, I don't hate you, how could I when I love you? We will cope with this together. I will never leave you, I promise. I have never been happier in my life than I have been since I found you. We will get through this. Now, dry your tears my love and be my brave girl."

"I can't believe I have found someone as wonderful as you. I'm so lucky," Marjorie smiled at him, even though smiling hurt her face a lot.

When Tony left her some time after, Marjorie felt better than she had in a very long time. She was glad that she now had nothing left to hide.

****

Tony visited Davey after he left his wife. He was so pleased to see him sitting downstairs in Sally's house looking much better and playing with Jess.

"Dad!" Davey was so happy to see him. "Look, this is Jess! Isn't she sweet?"

Tony sat down next to Davey and put his arm around his son. "She is indeed."

Sally's parents had gone home; they always had a rest after lunch. They had promised to return later and bring tea. Joe had gone home to report to his mum and get some fresh clothes. So Sally was alone with the two children.

"I think I'd better leave you two to have a talk," she said, picking up Jess. "Jess and I will just go for a walk; I could do with some fresh air for a while."

Tony smiled gratefully in thanks. When the young woman and her baby had gone out, he said to Davey: "Son, I want you to tell me exactly what happened that night. I want to know everything."

"Everything dad?" Davey looked at his father with his big brown eyes full of worry.

"Yes, son, everything. I want to know everything that Dickie did."

Davey hung his head; he was ashamed of what Dickie had done; it was dirty.

"It's all right, Davey; there is only we two here. Tell me."

So Davey told Tony in detail everything that had happened from the moment he knew someone was getting into his bed. Tony was furious; he contained himself with difficulty. If he could get his hands on Dickie now he would kill him - that was for certain. If only he could! As he listened, he felt proud of Marjorie, John and Davey. After all, they had all played a part: Marjorie came out in defence of Davey, John distracted Dickie in order to give Davey time to get the poker and climb on the bed - and Davey - In spite of being whipped, he somehow managed to get the strength to climb up and hit Dickie; what an incredible boy his was! Tony hugged his son and told him how proud he was of him.

"Now son, I want to hear about Marjorie; what has she been doing to you?"

Davey fell silent, not wanting to speak against her to his father. He shook his head. Tony gently undid a few of the buttons of the dressing gown and looked at his poor son's thin little body, his ribs sticking out like a starving child's; he realised that Davey was, indeed, a starving child. Davey quickly gathered the gown around himself, hanging his head. Tony put his hand under the lad's chin and made him look into his eyes.

"It's all right son; I know already, Marjorie has told me what she has done to you. I just wanted to see it for myself. She is so sorry for what she has done; do you think you may be able to forgive her one day?"

Davey looked into the eyes of his father, looked away and then nodded.

"I think she was very afraid of Uncle Dickie, dad. I think she was very brave to come and help me."

Tony felt a lump in his throat; where had he got this special boy from?

Sally came in with Jess then. She looked from father to son. She could feel the highly-charged emotion in the room.

"I will put the kettle on for a drink. I'm parched and I'm sure you two could do with a drink too?" and she went out of the room again. At that moment, Joe came in too and came into the kitchen to give her a kiss.

"Mum sends you her love," he said and sat down on a kitchen chair. "She has also sent Davey's clothes which she has washed and dried."

"Davey's dad is here," she informed him, "Jess and I have been out for a walk. I'm just making some tea. Do you want some?"

He nodded. "I will stay in here for a bit then. How is Davey?"

"He seems not at all bad now. You know what children are like, very sick one minute then they bounce up again! I'm going to put him in the bath; it hopefully will ease the sores on his back."

They went into the sitting room with the drinks and sat talking for a while. It helped to ease the atmosphere a bit and eventually Tony said he must be going.

"I have to go and see Marjorie again. She will be glad that Davey is so much better. Could I bring John to see Davey tomorrow?"

"Of course. You'd like to see John wouldn't you Davey?" she turned to Tony. "I would be glad if you could bring some of Davey's clothes, we only have one set for him just now."

"I will do that. Goodbye for now and thanks for everything."

*****

Marjorie was relieved to hear that Davey was getting better; she was also very upset when she heard about what Dickie had done but glad that Davey had resisted and fought back. He was such a brave little boy! How different to his attitude towards what she had done to him; he had become cowed and silent, hardly daring to be in her presence; just as she had been when she was being abused by her brother all those years ago. How could she not have seen it? How could she have done that to a little boy who did not deserve it? Didn't she know what it felt like? How cruel she was – now she just couldn't come to terms with what she had done; she was no better than Dickie. She talked at length with Tony, who just listened, his heart aching for his son and for her.

*****

The reunion between the two boys was a joy to see. John had missed his brother very much and was very glad to be with him again and grateful that he was safe.

"When are you coming home, Davey?" John asked hopefully.

"I'm afraid that Davey won't be coming home for a while yet," his father replied quietly. "He is not fully better yet and we have things that need to be sorted out."

"Can I come and live here with him then?" John looked from one adult to another. Tony looked stricken; he did not know what to say. They were living with Marjorie's parents at this time. Tony did not want to be in the house without Marjorie. Sally came to the rescue.

"Well, Mr. Adams, how about letting John come and stay here for a few days? There is a put-you-up bed in Davey's room so he could sleep in there. It will probably help Davey get better if his brother is with him. Just until you get sorted? Marjorie will probably need a bit of quiet when she comes out of hospital."

Tony looked at her gratefully. He knew there was going to be some difficult days ahead and it would be good to have John out of the way of it all, less upsetting....

"Thank you, Sally; you will never know how grateful I am for all you have done and all you are doing."

"I'm glad to be able to help, Mr. Adams. And you know that your sons will be safe and well looked after here."

"I do. Thank you."

Joe saw Mr. Adams to the door. Tony looked at Joe as he was about to go through the front doorway.

"Are you married to Sally?" he asked.

"No, but I hope to be before very long," was the reply.

"You have a good one there. Don't let her go."

"I agree. And, having lost her once and almost again, I intend not to let it happen again."

"Wise man - and a very lucky one." The two men shook hands and Tony went to face what he knew he must in support of the woman he loved.

Chapter 25

An Ending and Moving On

Marjorie was so glad to be able to leave the hospital and be at home with Tony again. They decided to go away for a few days in order to help her recover. They were supposed to be on holiday anyway, so they decided to go to their holiday destination. It wouldn't be the same without the boys, but Marjorie needed peace and quiet. She and Tony needed it to build a new understanding of each other. The sea air was therapeutic. It was beautiful weather too and it was all very healing for her, both outside and inside. She knew she would be facing some tough times when they got back. But she was also certain that Tony would stand by her and help her through.

True to her fears, the day after they came back home, the police came and arrested Marjorie for causing physical and mental abuse to Davey. They took her down to the station. Tony insisted on coming with her to wait in the station whilst they questioned her. He had arranged for her to have a solicitor with her. He was allowed to be with her for a few minutes before he had to leave her.

"Try not to worry love; I will never abandon you. And when they know about Dickie, I'm sure they will be lenient with you. You must tell them everything."

"I don't want to; I am ashamed."

"You must! They must see that you need help, not blame. I have already filled in Mr. Hill, your solicitor about all that. He will help you, my dear. Trust him, he is a good man."

"All right my love, I will try."

"Good girl." He kissed her. "I love you very much. Remember that."

The next day, Marjorie was given bail and allowed home. She was due to appear in court in two weeks' time.

****

Davey was asked to give evidence in court. He didn't want to do it; he didn't want to get Marjorie into trouble; he certainly didn't want her to go to prison. The kindly police inspector, Mr. Lock, who had spoken to John after the attack, came to Sally's house to see Davey there, along with a police woman.

"Davey, you know that we have photos that give evidence of what your stepmother has been doing to you. We want you to give evidence from behind a screen about what she did. Will you do it?

"Will she go to prison if I do that sir?"

"She might well. She will never be able to hurt you again, Davey."

"Then I won't do it, sir! I don't want her to go to prison; she is a very unhappy lady. And my daddy loves her; I don't want him to be sad because she will be in prison. And I can stay here with Auntie Sally for always, so mother won't hurt me anyway. I can stay with you always, can't I, Auntie Sally?" He looked at her pleadingly. She was so proud of him; he had been badly hurt but he didn't want to pay Marjorie back, or make his dad unhappy – what a very special boy he was!

"I certainly hope you can stay with me, Davey." She replied. "We will have to see what happens."

Inspector Lock was impressed with him too. He patted the boy on the head and turned to leave.

"You do know that Marjorie was abused by her brother, don't you, Inspector? And that he tried to assault Davey that night, but his intended victim was John, the younger brother?"

"Yes, I know about that, and, without Davey's say so, I doubt that she will get put into prison. We are investigating the man right now. A nasty piece of work I believe he is."

****

Marjorie's day in court was traumatic for all the family. When her solicitor brought out the information of how Dickie had sexually assaulted his sister for four years, her mother sat and cried, with Bill's arms around her, his face ashen. Davey sat and listened to the proceedings, his face pale as he watched Marjorie with her head lowered during this account. He recognised in her the same shame as he had felt, the same cowering submission that he had been through and his kind heart was sorry for her. He remembered how Dickie had hurt him and thought it must have been so bad for a little girl. At the summing up,

Davey found himself standing up with his hand in the air. The judge noticed him and asked why he had his hand up.

"Please sir, I'm Davey."

"You are?" the judge looked over his spectacles. "I was told you would not be in court today."

"I was not going to be, sir. But, I wondered if I could just say something, please?"

"Well young man, you will please come to the witness stand. We will hear what you have to say."

Davey moved to the stand. Everyone's eyes were on him, but he fixed his eyes on Sally to give him confidence. He took the oath and then turned to the judge.

"If you please sir, I would like to just say that I think that Uncle Dickie is a very bad man. And what he did to, to, mother, was terrible. He hurt me sir, but to hurt his little sister like that when he should have loved her was very bad indeed. I know how it feels, sir....." he gulped and looked then at Marjorie, who looked back at him with tears in her eyes. Then he turned back to face the judge.

"It's like this sir; I don't think mother is bad, 'cos she has looked after John and lots of other children at Beaumont House. And my dad wouldn't love her if she was bad. She is not bad sir, she is hurt. And when people are hurt they can sometimes do bad things. Uncle Dickie did something bad to me and I hit him very hard. I think mother needs to be helped so that she can feel better and get rid of how Uncle Dickie hurt her. I have Auntie Sally, who is helping me to get better. Mother needs daddy to get better. I don't want her to go to prison, sir."

There was a silence in the room; there were many people who were wiping tears from their eyes; the judge was very moved too. Davey went back to his seat besides Sally, who put her arms around him and hugged him.

"I'm so proud of you!" she whispered.

Marjorie was found guilty of causing grievous bodily harm to Davey Adams and was given a twelve months suspended sentence. The judge said that it was Davey's statement, together with the evidence of the brutal treatment from her brother that had saved her from prison. Davey was not allowed to live with her again but she could have supervised access, if Davey himself wished it.

Some time after the trial, Tony Adams came to see Sally. He told her that his work had offered him a job abroad for a while and he was proposing to take Marjorie with him. They had decided that they wanted to get rid of the house; when they came back they would buy another one that had no associations. In the meantime, would Sally consider having John as well as Davey while they were abroad, as they felt the boys should be kept together? He would pay her for John's keep.

The two families had been through a struggle, as the local authority had once again put Davey into care for his protection and wanted to put him back in Beaumont House. Tony, Sally, Sally's parents, Marjorie's parents and Emily Brown joined forces to convince the Child Care Officers that Davey was in the best place with Sally. Eventually, they relented and Sally went through the process of registering to become a foster carer. They didn't want to take her on at first because she was single, but, upon hearing that she was shortly going to marry Joe, they finally relented and let Davey stay.

So, the two boys were now living with Sally and attending Whitecross School, which was the secondary school in her area.

Joe had gone back home once Davey was better. He came every evening after work and stayed with her as long as possible, returning home when she went to bed. She really appreciated having him there every evening. He played with Jess after tea until she went to bed, then often sat and played with the boys, or played outside with them, playing football or other ball games. Sally would watch them through the window and feel really proud of her men folk.

She looked forward to the time when they would be married and Joe would be able to stay with her all the time.

****

It turned out that Dickie was wanted in several counties. He'd had quite a few different identities and he never stayed long in one place. He had a whole string of offenses, spanning about twenty years. They had arrested him as soon as he was fit enough to leave hospital and bail had been denied. He was held in Worcester prison while evidence was gathered from all over the country; it took several months to gather everything there was on him. There was also the evidence given by Marjorie and Davey. He was finally sentenced to thirty years. The judge said:

"You don't deserve to be let out on the unsuspecting world ever again. It goes beyond understanding how a young man can do such atrocities to his own sister. It is appalling that you could do such things to tiny children who are helpless and unable to tell anyone. Some you could have damaged physically forever. It is thanks to one very brave boy that you have finally been caught up with – that, and your complete inability to control yourself. You made a fatal mistake in attacking the family of the sister you abused for so long. You thought you could do anything you wanted; that you had complete control over her. That was your undoing. Now your reign of terror over her and other victims has ended. If I had my way, you would be locked up and the key thrown away, for the rest of your life."

Margaret and Bill were extremely distressed when they learned the truth about their two children. It was so hard to come to terms with the fact that their son could do such things to his little sister right under their noses and they had no idea; also it went beyond their understanding that Marjorie could do what she had done to Davey.

****

When the date for Sally and Joe's wedding was set, Maureen and Jim came to visit once evening. They had a proposal for them.

"It's like this, Sally and Joe, your dad and I feel that now we are on our own that Manvers is really too big for us. It seems rather silly that we are rattling around in a large house like that when there are five of you crammed into this little house. We wondered if you would like to move into Manvers? It's a wonderful place for children to grow up – lots of space. And you might well have more children..."

Sally and Joe looked at each other – goodness! They never expected this!

"But mum, you love Manvers! How could you bear to leave it?"

"Well, I do love it; but it is too much now – and the garden is too big for your dad."

"Thing is, the cottage down the lane is up for sale and it's going quite cheap as it has not been modernised for many years," explained Jim. "It would be much better for us and I would still be near work – and your mam would still be able to pop over to Manvers easily when you want her."

Sally and Joe decided they would indeed like to live at Manvers. The two boys were enthusiastic about it too – Davey loved it there and John did too. They often visited and spent Sundays there. They looked forward to it with enthusiasm.

Epilogue

Sally and Joe were married on a bright day at the beginning of April. It was a simple wedding; Sally wore a pretty dress and matching coat in a lovely pink, which enhanced the colour in her face. Jess looked sweet in a frilly white dress and had a little basket of flowers, which very soon suffered a nasty fate but not until after the photos had been taken! The church was decorated with arrangements full of bright daffodils, Sally's favourite flowers.

The reception was held at Manvers and was a small gathering of Sally's parents, her sister and her husband, Joe's mum, his brothers and their wives, Davey and John, Emily and Arthur Brown, Lillian and Andrea. It was a very happy occasion and Sally had no fears about the future as she had the first time round; she couldn't wait to start her life with Joe.

She and Joe went away for a few days to the Gower for a honeymoon, whilst Maureen and Jim took care of the three children.

They returned in a few days to affect the move to Manvers. Maureen and Jim had already more or less moved into the cottage down the lane. The house in Holly Avenue was sold. Everything had been packed before they went away. The removal van was bringing everything to Manvers that day. Sally's furniture was hardly sufficient for the big house, but her parents had left some of their larger bits that wouldn't fit into the cottage. And anyway, Joe and Sally would gradually decorate the house and buy other things of their own.

Later that day, they were all busy unpacking boxes and putting things away. John was keeping Jess entertained while Davey was helping Sally to unpack the box with her precious ornaments in. Joe was in the process of putting her little shelves on the wall ready to put them on. Davey was picking things out of the box and carefully unwrapping them and Sally was putting them on the mantle, to wait for Joe to finish putting the shelves up. Davey lifted something out of the box and held it up.

"Oh look Aunty! It's that tiger I gave you! He's not really an ornament; do you want him up there?"

"Yes dear, I do. Do you remember the day you gave him to me?"

"Yes. I paid sixpence to play the game and I got the tiger. I wanted to give you something to show you I loved you. I used to wish that you were my mother and I could be with you for always. My wish has come true and I will be with you for ever."

Sally hugged him.

"Well love, you will be with me until you grow up and leave to live a life of your own. But the tiger will remain with me for ever because it will always remind me of you and how I love you and you love me, even when I am very old! That tiger represents how love can help us overcome our problems; we just have to believe."

"I think I am the luckiest boy ever because I found you again, Aunty Sally! And you have made everything better for me."

"And I am lucky too because you found me Davey! And I am also lucky because you brought Joe back to me and he makes me happy too."

At that moment, Jess came to Joe and put her arms up for him to pick her up. He held her in one arm and put his hand out to stroke Sally's cheek. He smiled at Davey and said:

"Well, we are all lucky! I think that we have all got a lot of value out of that sixpence, matey!"

Other books by Jeanette Taylor Ford:

Rosa (A psychological thriller)

Elizabeth Fulton's grandfather, Lord Carrington, invites her to manage his country estate. Together they reopen her great-grandmother Rosa's long locked and abandoned bedroom and afterwards Elizabeth experiences some very strange and scary 'dreams', leading her to doubt everyone around her and her own sanity.

Bell of Warning

When Jeanie Turner starts 'seeing' the mysterious Kendra and the village of Shipden, which has lain under the sea off the coast of Cromer for five centuries, she wonders what is going on and what it will mean for her and her new husband and family.

The Hiraeth (Castell Glas Trilogy Book 1)

Shelly Richardson, who was abandoned as a baby, finds her family with the help of a ghostly aunt and two modern-day witches, unaware of lurking danger.

Coming soon:

Bronwen's Revenge (Castell Glas Trilogy Book 2)

The wicked Bronwen is dead, but that doesn't stop her wreaking revenge on those who thwarted her.

About the Author.

Jeanette Taylor-Ford is a retired Teaching Assistant. She grew up in Cromer, Norfolk and moved to Hereford with her parents when she was seventeen. An undiagnosed Coeliac, Jeanette was a delicate child and missed great deal of schooling, but she had one natural ability – even when only nine or ten she could write good stories. When young her ambition was to be a journalist but life took her in another direction and her life's work has been with children – firstly as a nursery assistant in a children's home, and later in education. In between she raised her own six children and she now has seven grandchildren.

Jeanette took up writing again in 2010; she reasoned that she would need something to do with retirement looming, although as a member of the Church of Jesus Christ of Latter Day Saints she is kept busy. She lives with her husband Tony, a retired teacher and headmaster, in Nottinghamshire, England.

13696914R00147

Printed in Great Britain
by Amazon.co.uk, Ltd.,
Marston Gate.